The TEA MAGIC Compendium

Create Your Own Brews and Herbal Potions While
Discovering the Grounding Power of Tea Witchcraft

~

Including 150 Recipes to Please and Serve

Phoebe Anderson

Copyright 2022 © by Phoebe Anderson

All rights reserved.

The content contained within this book may not be reproduced, duplicated, or transmitted without direct written permission from the author or the publisher.

Under no circumstances will any blame or legal responsibility be held against the publisher, or author, for any damages, reparation, or monetary loss due to the information contained within this book. Either directly or indirectly.

Legal Notice.

This book is copyright protected. This book is only for personal use. You cannot amend, distribute, sell, use, quote, or paraphrase any part, or the content within this book, without the consent of the author or publisher.

Disclaimer Notice.

Please note the information contained within this document is for educational and entertainment purposes only. All effort has been executed to present accurate, up-to-date, and reliable, complete information. No warranties of any kind are declared or implied. Readers acknowledge that the author is not engaging in the rendering of legal, financial, medical, or professional advice. The content within this book has been derived from various sources.

Please consult a licensed professional before attempting any techniques outlined in this book.

By reading this document, the reader agrees that under no circumstances is the author responsible for any losses, direct or indirect, which are incurred as a result of the use of the information contained within this document, including, but not limited to, errors, omissions, or inaccuracies.

First Printing Edition, 2022

Printed in the United States of America

Available from Amazon.com and other retail outlets

Table of Contents

~

Introduction, 5

Part 1. Tea Magic

Tea Witchcraft, 9
The Tea Making Process, 13
Tea Correspondence, Magical & Healing Proprieties, 19
Tea Blending, 25

Part 2. Potions & Brews

Moonbrews, 41
Emotional Healing, 44
Positiviteas, 45
Self-Love Potions, 49
Energy Healing, 52
Nighttime, 56
Everyday Potions, 58
Libido & Pleasure, 66
Friendship & Love, 67

Cold Brews, 69
Cozy Teas, 72
Morning Brews, 75
Tea with a Witch, 77
Witchy Brews, 79
Wheel of the Year, 87
Elixiers, 91
Spiritual Baths, 98

Conclusion, 99

Tea Recipes & Spells Index, 100

From the Author, 103

~

Introduction

Being a witch entails seeking the Great Wisdom. In searching for your path, you might come across different practices and have a hard time choosing which ones are right for you. The one piece of advice I can give you is this: follow your heart and your intuition. Whether you picked up this book because you want to know more about tea or because you feel like this is your calling, you're still walking your path towards enlightenment. I believe that ancient knowledge was passed down to us through the tea and herbs our ancestors used. Tea has been there since the beginning of humanity and has been used for various purposes. Therefore, using tea and herbs for their magical and medicinal properties is a way of honoring our ancestors. It's also a way to honor Mother Nature, who gives us these herbs to help us heal.

Tea is a powerful tool that can be utilized in magic, and in recent years people have rediscovered its magical properties. Tea magic is also a form of spiritual self-care. In this book, I aim to give you a comprehensive guide into tea and tea magic that'll tell you all you need to know about how to incorporate it into your spiritual practice. But before I do that, I need to talk about what spiritual self-care is. Personal responsibilities, empathy for others, and the pandemic can make you forget about yourself and your own needs. As a result, you may feel disconnected from the Divine, uninspired, and out of magic. But practicing spiritual self-care helps you create and maintain a connection with the Higher Power and nurture your spirit, and it can be practiced both inside and outside the context of religion. That is, if you're already part of a religion, you can incorporate it into your existing religious practices. If you aren't already following a religion, you can practice spiritual self-care independently.

Since spiritual self-care connects us with our true self, there are many benefits to it and many reasons to practice it, namely it'll:

* Encourage introspection and clarity.
* Improve your physical health and deepen your relationship with the self.
* Give you a sense of purpose or belonging.
* Improve your interpersonal relationships.
* Offer inner peace.

* Diminish feelings of isolation and loneliness, while enhancing oneness and universality.
* Help you connect with your intuition.
* Give you an insight into what makes you happy.
* Ground you.

But where does tea fit into spiritual self-care? Our ancestors have used tea for both medicinal and spiritual purposes. Tea is a great tool that helps you nourish your body, mind, and spirit. As part of your spiritual self-care routine, tea will give you the opportunity to establish a deep connection with Mother Gaia and your roots. Moreover, it has the same benefits as spiritual self-care. Having said that, the next chapter will discuss how tea is connected to spirituality and witchcraft.

Part 1

Tea Magic

"There is something in the nature of tea that leads us into a world of quiet contemplation of life."
— Lin Yutang, The Importance of Living

As always with holistic botanical witchcraft do your research to see if there are any reasons for you not to consume them.

Tea Witchcraft

Meditation, magic, and offerings to deities are ancient practices that are still used today. They help you strengthen and maintain your connection with the Source and are an integral part of worshiping the Divine. Back in 1,000 B.C.E. the Chinese drank tea for medicinal purposes and, later, on social occasions, too. Then, in 900 C.E., tea was incorporated in Buddhist ceremonies and rituals in Japan. Ever since, tea has been used for ceremonial purposes in many religions and is still used today as a self-care practice. In the next pages you'll learn about the different practices in which tea can be incorporated, including meditation, magic, and offerings.

TEA MEDITATION

Making and drinking tea helps with contemplation and listening and is a form of meditation. Drinking it helps you relax and offers you clarity or time for meditative contemplation. Utilizing tea in ceremonies, spells, and rituals is another way to meditate and a great addition to your spiritual routines. Alternatively, you can use it in infusions and potions with the intention of manifesting or creating. Plus, you can combine two enjoyable activities in one: meditating and drinking tea. Enjoying a cup of tea mindfully puts you in a meditative state instantly, since it makes you calmer. Moreover, tea meditation can give you a sense of peace and gratitude. After meditating with tea for some time, you'll observe that every time you're drinking tea, you enter this meditative state more easily, meaning that it'll be easier each time.

By extension, you'll be able to induce this state without the tea, as being aware will become a habit for you. To do it:

- Breathe deeply and remind yourself that this is a time to clear your mind.
- After you feel like you're fully present, pick your favorite tea or the one that has the properties you want to heal/achieve (more on the different properties of tea in Chapters 3 and 4).
- Pour water into a kettle and try to focus on the sound of the boiling water.
- Put the tea of your choice in the mug and focus your awareness on your bodily movements during this process.
- Pour the boiling water into the mug and infuse the tea. Take a few breaths and focus on how the color of the water changes.
- After it's infused, remove the tea leaves or the bag from the water and deeply inhale the vapors.
- Show gratitude, by giving thanks to the tea, yourself, and the universe.
- For each sip you're taking, allow yourself to remain in this calm state.

Additionally, tea meditation can be focused on the specific result you want to achieve. This way you can have more effective results.

Meditating for inner calm and happiness helps you feel more relaxed and content. To do this, prepare your tea as indicated above and go to your favorite room or place. Hold the cup in your hands, close your eyes, and breathe in. Take the time to breathe in the steam, focus on its smell, and notice the sensation in your lungs. When breathing out, imagine you're releasing any tension, stress, or negative energy. Repeat this a few times and imagine that every time you breathe in, positive energy enters your body. If you want to heal some part of your body, you can concentrate your healing energy there. With every sip, focus on the warmth it gives you and feel the positive energy flowing throughout your body.

Additionally, you can also meditate with tea to declutter your mind and your thoughts, which will give you a clearer mind. Again, prepare the tea as above, close your eyes, and focus on your breath. Inhale for four seconds, hold for three seconds, exhale for six seconds, and repeat ten times. While you're doing this, imagine you're in a place you love and think about all the sensations you can feel (e.g. the smell of flowers, the sensation of the wind on your skin, the colors of the sky, the sound of the waves, etc.). When you're inhaling, feel the energy everywhere in your body. When you're exhaling, imagine all the unwanted thoughts leaving your body. Repeat this as many times as necessary, until you feel relaxed. After you do this, thank your tea and Mother Nature and come back to the present slowly.

TEA AND MAGIC

As I've said before, it's a wonderful idea to add tea into the practices of witchcraft, but it's important to do this the right way. Therefore, here you can find a few tips to maximize your results or avoid negative effects. First, it's essential to add intention to your ingredients and inform the brew of what you're trying to accomplish. You can set your intention while steering the brew clockwise (for invocations) or counterclockwise (for banishing) and finish the process with the phrase 'as I will, so mote it be.' Each tool you're using works like a magical tool. For instance, the spoon is a wand, the pot works like a cauldron, etc. Adding honey will sweeten your tea spells and using moon water will make them more potent. As you can see, the process of making tea can work like any other spell. This means that

you can prepare the tea in this way and then consume it mindfully as discussed before.

However, you need to research the plant or herb you are consuming, as some herbs can have negative effects on certain conditions. This will help you get to know each herb and create an herbal routine that's suitable for your body. Knowing the magical correspondences of the herb you're choosing is a very important factor to achieve the desired results. So, essentially, you're doing three different things at the same time:

* Casting a spell.
* Meditating.
* Healing your body through the herb's medicinal properties.

On that note, you also need to consider whether the herb you're intending to consume can be combined with medication you're already on, since it's known that some teas counteract medication or amplify them. You'll also need to know which herbs don't react well with metal, because most kettles, pans, and spoons are made with metal. Furthermore, you should let the tea steep for 15 minutes, because this way it'll be stronger. You should also find out which time of day it's best to consume each herb, as some of them work better during the morning and others at evening. Some blends contain more caffeine than others, so, for example, you don't want to consume a blend that contains a lot of caffeine at nighttime, because it might cause insomnia and disturb the circadian rhythm.

TEA AS AN OFFERING

Tea can be a great offering to God and Goddess, and this practice has been around since ancient times. Offerings are a way of showing gratitude to the deity for what they've given to you. These gifts strengthen your partnership with the God or Goddess. There's an abundance of historical texts to read about what teas our ancestors offered to their deities that were grown in their lands. For example, ancient Egyptians offered catnip to Bastet. Since Bastet was a Goddess associated with fertility, sex, and love, it makes sense that the ancient Egyptians offered her catnip, which is associated with prosperity and abundance. You can do the same and offer your deity some tea that's native to the land where they were once worshiped or an herb that has the same correspondences as your deity. You can start by researching the native plants of the deity's area. Keep in mind that you can use more than one herb at the same time for an offering. So, after you've decided which herbs you'll offer, there are many options in using them. Namely, you can:

* Put them in hot water and offer them as tea.
* Prepare them in a ritual, as described in the previous section.
* Charge them in moonlight and choose the appropriate Moon phase, depending on what you want to achieve, for maximum results.
* Set them on your altar.
* Pour yourself a cup too and drink some at the same time as you are offering it.

To illustrate the process of offering tea to a deity, I'm going to talk about two deities. First, Hecate is the ancient Greek Goddess of the witches. You can make tea for her by researching the herbs associated with her. If you can't find any, look up plants that were native to ancient Greece. Moreover, it's

known that the pomegranate is her sacred fruit, which means that it should be included in the tea. Another ingredient you might want to include is lavender, as it's associated with warding off evil spirits and purifying. Peppermint is associated with prophetic dreams, cleansing, and protection, which makes it the perfect ingredient if you want to invoke her to help you enhance your psychic abilities. Furthermore, black is the color associated with Hecate, and black tea works ideally as a color association. You can say an incantation before drinking or offering it.

Secondly, Apollo is an ancient Greek sun-God. To make a tea for Apollo you can start with chamomile, which is directly associated with the sun. You can also use yellow tea, because yellow is associated with Apollo and the sun. Honey is also consistent with Apollo's color association, as well as with abundance and prosperity. Lastly, you can add some cinnamon, which corresponds to luck and prosperity. At this point you can recite an incantation if you wish. With that said, there are many more ingredients that are consistent with the color association (yellow) and properties (luck, abundance, prosperity) of Apollo, which you can find online. So, now that you've learned about how to use tea for meditation, magic, and offerings, it's time to share with you the process of making tea, as well as the different blends out there and how you can use them.

The Tea Making Process

Fairytales are filled with witches stirring cauldrons and making potions. Sometimes, these are poisons or are used to help the protagonist achieve their goal. Nowadays, with the rise of spiritual practices, potions have become part of many people's spiritual routines. But what is a potion, you might ask? Well, it's a liquid mixture made of many ingredients that vary according to the desired result. Since ancient times, people have been making potions for spiritual purposes. A potion can be consumed by the person who made it, given to another person to consume, or offered to a deity. Moreover, regardless of their purpose, potions were and still are a part of rituals sometimes. The person who's making the potion does so in a ceremonial way by chanting or casting a spell, depending on their spiritual practices. And how is a potion different from any other liquid mixture? Potion-making is a spiritual practice in which the ingredients added to the mixture have a spiritual significance. The spiritual significance of the ingredients has to do with the number of ingredients in it, which can correspond to a deity or the result you want to achieve, and the color and astrological associations of the ingredients (corresponding to a deity, season, or desired result), among others. The tools you're using to make the potions are the same as those outlined in the chapter called 'The Tea-Making Process' and can be as fancy or as simple as you want.

Considering that the potion-making process looks a lot like casting a spell, you need to start with your intent. To achieve the best possible results, your intent needs to be specific. I'm sure that most practitioners of magic have a story to tell you about how their intention wasn't specific enough during a ritual or a spell, and they ended up with a very different result than they hoped for. Let's say that, for example, you're making a potion or casting a spell to attract money. If your intention isn't specific enough, like 'I want to gain money', then you might end up stumbling upon a $1 bill. Therefore, it's better if you're specific, like 'I want $200,' and let the universe take it from there. Keep in mind that your intention should be achievable. For instance, if you ask for $1,000,000 or to be able to teleport, it isn't very likely that you'll get it. Finally, you should also consider the ethical side of your intention. Now, I'm aware that this is a controversial issue in the New Age community and that people have very strong opinions on this subject. What I'm suggesting here is just that you need to consider if the intention you're setting is consistent with your code of ethics.

Making tea mindfully is key if you want to use it for magical purposes. But it's also important to know practical information about which tea blend you should pick, depending on what you want to achieve. You can research the medicinal properties of tea too, but here you'll learn about its magical properties. Furthermore, combining herbs together can help you achieve your desired outcome. To do that, you can combine the knowledge you will get in the coming chapters to make teas that are suitable for your needs and practices. That's why making tea is such a personal practice: There are countless herbs out there and countless combinations you can make that are right for your soul, spirit, and body.

There are so many ways to make your tea more magical, including:

* Match the color of your cup to your intention.
* Stir clockwise to manifest or invoke.
* Stir counterclockwise to banish or repel.
* Tap the spoon against the rim of the mug three times to seal an intention.
* The day of the week you're making it.
* The properties and correspondences of the herbs you are putting in.
* The deity you're offering it to.
* The phase of the Moon on the day you're making it.
* The season you're making it, according to the Wheel of the Year.
* The number of herbs you're putting in.
* The color of the herbs, which can correspond to a deity or season.
* Charging it by moonlight or sunlight.
* Making the preparation process into a ritual.
* Your zodiac sign or the sign in which the moon is at the time you're making it.

In this book I'll discuss various recipes for different magical purposes, like grounding, banishing, luck, prosperity, and abundance, among others, that can be used as part of your spells and rituals, or before casting a spell. It's important to note that there are many ways of enchanting your tea.

Since magic is a personal practice, it looks different for everyone. Therefore, feel free to adjust the recipes/practices presented here to accommodate your own practice.

MAGICAL TEA TOOLKIT

To make drinking tea more magical, you should have a few necessary tools at hand. Now, these tools can be as expensive or as fancy as you want, or they can be everyday items you already own. It's definitely up to you. In this section I'll explain what you need to enchant your tea and incorporate it into your practice:

Grimoire. In all magical practices, a grimoire is very important because that's where you store all knowledge. This can be a regular notebook, where you can write your spells and tea recipes. You can also write about your 'experiments,' meaning that you can record which herbal combinations work and which ones don't, so that you know what to repeat and what to avoid. A grimoire will give you the chance to reflect on your spell work and remember which spells work best. Plus, it works as a journal, which you can look back at to review your progress.

Tea Infuser. This is pretty much self-explanatory, as you need a tea infuser to infuse your herbs and keep the blend together.

Storage Containers. Apart from the herbs and teas, you'll also need to decide where you're going to store them. Glass vials, mason jars, and zip lock bags are great ways to store your herbs. However, the thing that matters the most is that the container is airtight and that it's stored in a dark and cool place. More on storing herbs later in this section.

Teacup and Saucer. You can use any teacup or mug that you like and feel at home with.

Spoon. Any kind of spoon is fine, but there are many choices. If you want, you can buy a spoon with sigils on it or with a crystal at the handle. There are many spoons to choose from at your local witchy store.

Mortar and Pestle. If you want to grind up your herbs, you can use a mortar and pestle.

Internet Access. There are so many spells and recipes on the internet, which you can find and modify to your needs.

These are pretty much all you need to start off. Feel free to modify this list according to your needs or add more items to your liking.

SOURCING HERBS

It's widely recognized that locally grown herbs are the best. That's because the place in which the herbs are grown makes them slightly different in terms of flavor, color, and potency. Therefore, if the herb you're buying is grown in your area, it's accustomed to the same weather, climate, and seasons as you are, and will work better in your body. Plus, you'll be supporting your small, local shops and producers. Keep in mind that locally grown products might be slightly more expensive, as they're of higher quality. This means that they'll be fresher and more potent, compared to those that have been imported. However, sometimes the herbs you're looking for might not be able to grow in your region and you'll have to buy them from overseas. Unfortunately, many herbs that are native to tropical and subtropical areas come from developing countries and are produced by child or forced labor, or by exploitation of labor. In these cases, it's best to thoroughly research the seller or buy from local stores that you know take these ethical concerns very seriously.

METHODS OF PREPARATION

The appropriate way to prepare tea depends on the part of the plant you're using (i.e. flower, seed, bark, leaf, stem, etc.) and which properties you want to extract. Mainly, there are two ways to prepare tea:

Infusion

This is the most common and well-known method of making tea. Infusion is a process with water as the main solvent, in which water is poured over the herbs to extract their properties. In infusion, you usually put one or two tablespoons of herbs for every one and a half cup of water. However, you can change this ratio depending on how strong you like your tea. This method is ideal for flowers, leaves, and soft berries. These parts need to be left in the water for a short time only, as they might lose their constituents. Additionally, infusion and decoction are suitable for barks and stems. There are many tools you can use that are widely available to prepare a hot or cold infusion, such as mason jars, teapots, a French press, or a teacup with a lid. Remember that infusions can be stored for up to 24 hours.

Hot Infusion

To prepare a hot infusion, you can follow the aforementioned ratio of one or two tablespoons of herbs per one and a half cup of water. After you boil the water and pour it over the herbs, let it steep for about 15 to 20 minutes. For black and green tea, steep for five minutes.

Cold Infusion

To prepare a cold infusion, you need one tablespoon of tea per cup of water. Pour the water inside a lidded jar, along with the tea, shake, and store for two hours in a cool place. This method is suitable for extracting enzymes, mucilaginous carbohydrates, flavonoids, and vitamins.

Decoction

This method involves slowly bringing to boil seeds, stems, barks, and roots, by placing them in a pot with cold water and heating them up. These parts lose some of their properties in hot water, so it is important that they boil slowly. Decoction involves using a lidded saucepan and pouring in one cup of water and one tablespoon of tea. Once the water starts to boil, reduce the heat, and leave it there for 20 to 45 minutes. When the time is up, remove from the heat and strain.

Witch's Brew

You can make your own potion or brew, using tea, that incorporates all five of the alchemical elements and intention. This means that your brew will be more powerful. With water being the main medium, you can include flowers, roots, leaves, fruit, and seeds in your brew to represent earth. The steam and the way the tea smells are associated with air, while the warmth it transmits on your hands represents fire. The Spirit involves combining all these elements and consuming the tea mindfully. Moreover, another great idea to make your tea more magical is to take numerology into account, by deciding the number of different herbs you'll add depending on what you want to achieve. For example, three is a magical number, so you can have one main herb plus two supporting herbs.

So, the first thing you need to do is set your intention. The second step is to choose your main herb, which represents the main purpose of your brew, and then choose the supporting herbs that will enhance it. You can determine this by their taste, fragrance, correspondences, color, and tradition-

al uses. For instance, if you have digestive issues caused by anxiety, peppermint is a great option as your main herb. It's also associated with strengthening the solar plexus, which will give you more confidence and the ability to uncover inner knowledge. In this brew, you can add Earl Gray and ginger, which strengthens the solar plexus. Regarding measurements, you'll need about one teaspoon of dried herbs per cup of tea. To make this tea:

1. Take three sprigs of mint and pluck the leaves.
2. Put them in the infuser and add a few grates of fresh ginger, as well as a teaspoon of Earl Gray.
3. Speak an incantation, if you wish.
4. Add boiling water to a cup, cover, leave it for five minutes, and strain.
5. You can speak your incantation again, while you're drinking it.

BREWING TIMES AND TEMPERATURES

Though most teas will make a decent cup if you steep them all in boiling water, every type of tea has an optimum time range for steeping and a preferred water temperature for brewing that allows maximum flavor without bitterness. Using too hot water, you could burn delicate tea leaves, resulting in an unpleasant, bitter cup. Using too cool water, you risk ending up with a weak, less flavorful cup of tea. Let's be specific here: I refer to loose leaf tea–not bagged tea. When it comes down to tea bags, the temperature of water you're using doesn't matter.

Young teas like green or white tea should be treated gently. They have more delicate flavor compounds and should be brewed with lower temperature water. Black teas are the most robust tea variety and can be brewed in boiling water. While teas that have been fermented, like oolong, fall between green and black. The best temperature to extract the complex flavors is less than black tea and it should be steeped longer than green tea. There are so many different herbs that can be brewed for herbal tea, that there is no way to give any steeping guidelines or temperature with any accuracy. Generally, most herbs can be brewed in boiling water and steeped for about 5 minutes. One exception is Roobois, a full-bodied red herbal tea from South Africa that should be prepared with fully boiling water, just like black tea.

The tea steeping times below are approximate, and you should adjust them depending on your tea taste. You might need a bit of trial to get the perfect brew.

* **Black tea:** Temperature: 205-212°F (96-100°C) - Time: 3-5 minutes
* **White tea**: Temperature: 175-180°F (79-82°C) - Time: 3-4 minutes
* **Green tea**: Temperature: 175-180°F (79-82°C) - Time: 2-3 minutes
* **Oolong tea**: Temperature: 180-195°F (79-82°C) - Time: 2-3 minutes
* **Pu-erh**: Temperature: 195-200°F (90-95°C) - Time: 4-5 minutes
* **Yellow**: Temperature: 175-180°F (79-82°C) - Time: 2-3 minutes

If you don't have a thermometer, you can tell the water temperature by watching the bubbles. You can see strings of bubbles from the bottom of the kettle at 180 to 190° F., and small bubbles will float to the surface of the water 160 to 170° F.

STORING YOUR HERBS

Storing your herbs and teas properly is very important if you want them to retain their potency, fragrance, medicinal properties, and flavor. Teas and herbs should be kept away from heat, moisture, and light. For instance, a cabinet is great for storing your herbs and teas, as it protects them from light, moisture, and heat. You can also store them in a container, and if you're storing them correctly, the type of container doesn't matter at all.

To conclude, in this chapter you've learned about sourcing and storing herbs, as well as how to make tea, brews, and the tools you're going to need. This is a crucial first step to using tea for magical purposes and, in the next chapter, I'm going to discuss the different teas, herbs, and spices that are available in the market.

Tea Correspondence, Magical & Healing Proprieties

Before I discuss the different teas, herbs, and spices it's important to remember that, if you're doing tea magic, these are your tools. This means that they should be treated with respect and be cared for properly. Furthermore, since these herbs and spices will be consumed one way or another, be it in food, teas, or scented candles, you need to know about them before consuming them. That's because they might cause various negative effects, depending on each person's body and needs. Some of these negative effects include causing allergic reactions, interacting negatively with existing health conditions, and counteracting medication you're already on, among others. Therefore, it's important to research each plant before you consume it or consult a health professional, so that you're sure that it's the right choice for you. With that said, in this chapter you'll find descriptions for different herbs, teas, and spices. You can buy all of these in local witch shops, farmers markets, and grocery stores, or even grow them yourself, if this is something you like to do.

In this chapter we are going to learn about the different herbs, teas, and spices and their magical and healing proprieties, which will help you understand the different blends and teas I'll share with you in the following chapter like green tea, black tea, hibiscus tea, lemon balm, and rooibos, along with recipes for chakra healing and astrological correspondences. There is a slew of herbs used in cooking that also have magical uses, and you probably have many of them in your cupboard at this very moment.

The Elements in Tea Magic

Air: The arising steam makes tea a dream
Fire: The Internal heat is a blesses treat
Earth: The roots and leaves that make our teas
Water: The water we use to drink our brew
Spirit: The realmy connction with teatime reflection

~

Tea Correspondences

BLACK TEA

Gender: Masculine **Elements**: Fire **Crystal**: Obsidian
Planet: Mars **Season**: Winter **Color**: Black and red

Magical Properties: Courage, strength, banishing boredom, prosperity, money, mind stimulation

GREEN TEA

Gender: Masculine **Elements**: Fire **Crystal**: Malachite
Planet: Mars **Season**: Summer **Color**: Orange and green

Magical Properties: Health, love and passion, energy, cleansing, and money

WHITE TEA

Gender: Masculine **Elements**: Air and fire **Crystal**: Quartz
Planet: Mars and the Sun **Season**: Spring **Color**: White, yellow, and gold

Magical Properties: Cleansing, clarifying, aural health, psychic abilities, connection with Spirit, fertility, youth, and new beginnings

OOLONG TEA

Gender: Feminine **Elements**: Water **Crystal**: Amethyst
Planet: Mars and the Moon **Season**: Autumn **Color**: Purple and dark blue

Magical Properties: Love, serenity, reflection, divination, emotional balance

Common Herbal Tea Correspondences

Cream: Abundance, fertility, creativity, employment, happiness, health
Honey: Attraction, love, lust, sex magic, binding, improve someone's disposition, flu and cold treatment
Sugar: Love, sympathy, wisdom, attraction, improve someone's disposition

~

Basil: Love, wealth, blessing, flying, protection

Bay: Protection, psychic powers, healing, purification, strength

Bergamot: Protection from evil, illness, and magical interference

Calendula: Divination, remembrance, honor

Cardamom: Love and trust

Catnip: Love, beauty, happiness

Chamomile: Healing, abundance, receiving energy enhancement, sleep, purification

Chicory: Removing obstacles, invisibility, favors, frugality

Cinnamon: Spirituality, success, healing, power, psychic powers, lust, shielding, love

Clove: Protection, love, money

Dandelion Root: Dream magic, divination, spirit work

Dandelion: Wishes, divination, calling spirits, success

Dill: Protection, money, lust, sexual love

Eucalyptus: Cleansing, healing

Fennel: Protection, healing, purification

Garlic: Protection, healing, exorcism, lust, anti-theft

Ginger: Success, prosperity, confidence, sensuality, protection, beauty and love

Hibiscus: Independence, divination, dream magic confidence, strength, love, and passion

Honeysuckle: Prosperity and abundance

Jasmine: Love, dreams, luxury, sensuality, divination

Lemon Balm: Love, success, healing

Lemon: Cleansing, removing energy blockages

Lemongrass: Cleansing, opening the psychic mind

Mint: Money, lust, healing, travel, protection

Orange Peel: Luck and money

Peppermint: Purification, sleep, love, healing, psychic powers

Rooibos: Strength, courage, determination, patience

Rose Hips: Healing, good luck

Rosemary: Protection, love, lust, mental powers, purification, healing, sleep, youth

Sage: Immortality, longevity, wisdom, protection, cleansing, wishes

Thyme: Health, healing, sleep, psychic powers, love, purification, courage

Herbs for Higher Consciousness

Albizzia (Mimosa): Tree of eternal happiness. Attunes to the consciousness open the field to oneness.

Ashwagandha: Adaptogenic, rejuvenating, relates to the spirit.

Blue Lotus: Bluewater Lilly is a precious flower used ceremonially to assist deep states of meditation, euphoria, and relaxation.

Bobinsana: A stimulant native to the Amazon, known to boost, protect, and ground spiritual energy. Opens to the dream world and mystical worlds of nature.

Cacao: Helps to find the journey within, connect to our heart, reveal patterns, cultivate self-love, and increase consciousness.

Coca: A protective ally in the spiritual world that sharpens senses, stimulates, and rejuvenates.

He Shou Wu: Powerful rejuvenator, known in traditional Chinese medicine for its psychospiritual effects, classified as a shen and used as a yin tonic.

Holy Basil: Masterful adaptogen, bringer of joy and peace. Elevates and nourishes the "Vital Spirit."

Kratom: Disconnects the pain body and facilitates higher consciousness.

Mucuna: a.k.a. Dopamine bean. A consciousness enchanting plant that contains compounds that activate our pineal, pituitary, and hypothalamus glands. Contains a small amount of DMT.

Nutmeg: Stimulates the pineal gland, boots insight, clarity, and mental concentration.

Passion Flower: Its essence is known to repattern consciousness to attain wholeness again. The leaves help to relax and activate the parasympathetic nervous system.

Schisandra: Masterful adaptogen that powerfully regulates the limbic system (our emotional center) and endocrine system. Known to contain the three treasures, jing, qi, and shen.

Skullcap: Brings balance to the nervous system and helps to bring consciousness back to the body after astral projection.

Herbs with Strong Metaphysical Properties

Mint: Attracts good spirits and energy. Washing your front door with mint can bring abundance and protection.

Mugworth: Believed to increase natural psychic powers and induce astral projection. It has also been used for centuries to ward off evil spirits and energy.

Oregano: Removes negative energy and increases positivity. It can help us gain spiritual knowledge and reminds us to be humble.

Parsley: Believed to help people communicate with the other side. It is also believed to increase passion, vitality, and strength.

Rosemary Balm: Used to balance emotions and calm your mind. Using Lemon balm incense can induce sleep.

Thyme: It can cleanse your aura and home while bringing good luck and wealth. It is believed to bring courage and inner power.

Herbs for Emotional Trauma

Try adding white yarrow flower essence to your tea for an extra boost of energetic protection. White yarrow flower essence helps prevent those who are energetically sensitive from being drained by.

~

Cherry Blossom: Helps to release toxic fluids from the body, which is a necessary step to release emotional trauma. It supports kidney function.

Dandelion Root: A blood purifier, which benefits the function of the gallbladder, liver, kidney, and heart, organs that commands emotional processing.

Hawthorn: Improves a sense of calm, hope, and love. It helps blood circulation in the brain.

Lemon Balm: Balances the nervous system and clears the liver and heart. It calms the mind. If taken before bed may prevent nightmares.

Eleuthero Root: Helps cope with stressful situations, adaption to changes, create endurance, and enhance productivity during difficult times.

Nettle Leaf: Promotes good blood circulation, clearing the kidneys where fears are physically stored. It helps soothe anger.

Herbs for Emotional Balance

Oatstraw: Supports the nervous system and has a mild flavor making it easy to blend with most herbs in teas

Nettle Leaf: A nutritive herb that helps improve the body's resistance, nourishes and tones the veins, and cleanses the blood, supports the adrenals and the endocrine (hormone) glands.

Dandelion Root: A detoxifier that supports the liver and kidneys and helps to clear the body of stored negative emotions such as anger and fear. Dandelion is also supportive of both physical and emotional digestion.

Linden: Helps to calm the nerves and move stagnant energy.

Lavender: Helps to calm the body on a physical level and remove negative energies on a spiritual level.

Sage: An aromatic herb that helps promote mental alertness and soothes anxiety

Lemon Balm: Another wonderful herb for lifting the spirits. I didn't add this one to my tea blend because it's not recommended for those who have an underactive thyroid. If this is not an issue for you, I highly recommend adding some lemon balm to your tea blends.

Herbs for Menthal Health

Try to add The Bach flower remedy White Chestnut to your tea, which is available from most food shops, can help to soothe a mind troubled with repetitive thoughts. It is used primarily to ease mental agitation and worry, thus aiding restful sleep.

~

Camomile: Relieves anxiety and helps you sleep.

Lavender: A sedative effect that soothes and calms nerves.

Saffron: Releases serotonin-producing feelings of positivity and happiness.

Green Tea: Improve mood, energy, and memory.

Passion Flower: Brain chemicals that produce a calming effect.

Lemon Balm: Treats anxiety and sleep disorders.

Turmeric: Releases serotonin and dopamine, giving happy feelings.

Healing Herbs for Women

Fennel: Fennel relieves gas, bloating and supports breast milk production.

Dong Quai: Balances hormones and estrogen. It can relieve PMS and menopause symptom.

Raspberry: Healthy menstruation, soothes cramps, tomes the uterus, prepares the womb for birth.

Black Cohosh: Hormone balance, helps with PMS and hot flashes.

Shatavari: Adaptogen, hormonal balance, rejuvenation, breast milk support.

Maca: Adaptogen, hormone nourisher, boosts libido and fertility, relieves menopausal symptoms.

Vitez: Regulates menses, hormonal balancer, and pituitary tonic.

Culinary Healing Herbs

Parsley: Fresh breath, antioxidant, vitamins K C A, digestive aid.

Chives: Mild diuretic, antibacterial, bug repellent.

Rosemary: Hair growth, antistress, improves memory.

Mint: Digestive aid, headache relief, nausea relief.

Fennel: Bloating relief, heartburn relief, eye health, lower blood pressure.

Thyme: Mood booster, sore throat relief, Vitamins A and C.

Basil: Pain relief, immune booster, blood vessel health, antioxidant.

Bay Leaf: Improves insulin function, minimizes candida, treats dandruff, antioxidant.

Tea Blending

Tea blending is the process of combining different teas together, according to the desired result. There are many reasons why people choose to combine teas, with one of them being flavor. Some teas have stronger flavor compared to others, which means that they might be very bitter or acidic. Therefore, you can add another herb that will break down the strength of their flavor to make them more enjoyable. Another reason to blend teas is for medicinal purposes because combining different plants together combines their medicinal properties to achieve a greater result. Additionally, sometimes, in order for a plant's medicinal properties to be released, it needs to be combined with other plants.

Moreover, blending different teas also has magical connotations for many different reasons, including:
* The number of herbs you're choosing to combine can correspond to your deity or the result you want to achieve.
* If you're working with color associations, then you can combine different herbs of the same color, corresponding to your deity, season, or desired result.
* If you're working with the zodiac circle, you can use plants associated with different signs.
* You might also want to combine the plants that are associated with the specific chakra you are working with.

So, the question is: *How do I choose which herbs to combine in my tea?* Well, I would say that it takes some time. First, it starts with reading and learning about the different teas and herbs, which you're already doing. Then, it requires a lot of experimenting. Even though there may be plenty of failed attempts, you'll gain a lot of valuable knowledge along the way. After all, you can't learn if you don't make mistakes. However, here you'll learn the basics of how to blend teas together. When you know about the basics, then you can venture off on your own and see which blends make sense for you, your needs, and your body.

With that said, the first thing you need to consider is whether you want a medicinal or a tasty tea. Having this in mind, you then need to think about your ingredients and their qualities in order to choose your basic ingredient and the supportive and complementary ones. The basic ingredient acts as the active component, and you should use three parts of it. Then, you'll use two parts of the sup-

portive and one part of the complementary components (e.g. for every three teaspoons of the basic ingredient, you'll add two teaspoons of the supportive, and one of the complementary components). After that, you need to ensure that they don't counteract each other's properties. For example, if you want to make culinary tea, you can use rooibos, green tea, or black tea as your base, and a combination of peppercorns, cinnamon, lemon and orange zest, or chamomile, rose, and lavender as your complementary ingredients. If you want a medicinal tea, the basic ingredients include calendula, echinacea, tulsi, linden, peppermint, or lemon balm; the supportive ingredients consist of lemon grass, thyme, rosemary, dandelion, yarrow, or linden; while the complementary ingredients are fennel, cinnamon, turmeric, lavender, or ginger.

As a practitioner of magic, it's often helpful to follow your instinct. Shamans and healers of the past didn't have the knowledge of medicine, biology, and chemistry we have today, and relied on experimentation and their intuition to find out the best combinations of plants. Even though today you have all the necessary knowledge, you may often get lost in the vastness of the internet and get confused as to what's the best option. Thus, you might find that relying on your intuition helps you find out the best combination for you. It's also important to document your 'experiments' each time so that you know what works. This way you won't repeat the same mistake over and over and will be able to change up your recipes to achieve the desired result. Finally, you need to know the brewing time and temperatures, so that you don't accidentally spoil your tea.

There are a few things you need to keep in mind when you're blending herbs and teas. Namely:

1. Your hands and equipment should be clean and dry, as moisture can spoil the herbs.
2. You should weigh one herb at a time before pouring it into the mix.
3. You need to blend your herbs slowly, either with your hands or using a spoon, so that they're mixed evenly.

Common Bases & Recipes

In the following section, I'll share with you the most common teas, with recipes for blends you can make at home. These recipes will demonstrate the basics of well-known bases, so that you'll know how to use them in your practice and which ingredients are best combined with each base. Moreover, these teas will act as the basic ingredient in most of the recipes you'll find in this book, and learning about them will also give you an idea of how to use them in your magical practice.

BLACK TEA

Black tea contains a lot of caffeine and is very stimulating, so you want to avoid it at nighttime or if you have trouble sleeping. However, the caffeine is absorbed slower than the caffeine in coffee, so it gives you a more gradual feeling of energizing. Black tea can be combined with cardamom, lavender, ginger, lemon zest, vanilla, cocoa nibs, tulsi, rose, licorice, or peppercorn, which can be used for grounding. To make a tea, combine one part black tea as your basic ingredient, with a pinch of peppercorns as the complementary ingredient, and one inch of ginger as the supportive ingredient, or one part black tea with half a part of rose as your supportive ingredient.

Rose Breakfast Blend

Stronger and lighter teas are combined in this blend and, as the name suggests, it's a perfect addition to your breakfast. It also goes very well with milk, and if you want to increase the caffeine level, you can add guarana powder. To make this blend, you'll need to combine:

* Assam tea (three teaspoons)
* Darjeeling tea (two teaspoons)
* Rose buds (half a teaspoon)

Tropical Pu-erh Blend

Since pu-erh has a strong, earthy flavor, it's better if combined with fruit. You can choose other fruits or adjust the ratio to your liking or blend it with fruit tea. To make this blend, mix the following:

* Pu-erh tea (two tablespoons)
* Candied pineapple, candied mango, and shredded coconut (a teaspoon each)

Chai Blend

Chai is usually consumed with milk and many different spices. The spices need to be crushed in a mortar. Apart from the ingredients mentioned below, you can also add vanilla, cocoa shells, nutmeg, and star anise to the blend:

* Assam black tea (three to five tablespoons)
* Cloves, cardamom, dried ginger (a teaspoon each), and a cinnamon stick of about two inches
* Peppercorns (half a teaspoon)

GREEN TEA

Green tea gives you a gradual energy boost and is good for digestive problems and an upset stomach. It can be combined with jasmine, peppermint, lemon balm, lemon grass, rose, and lavender. It can be used for energizing. To make a tea, you can combine two parts of green tea as the basic ingredient with half a part lemon zest as your complementary ingredient, and one part peppermint and one part lemongrass as your supportive ingredients. Other ingredients that mix well with green tea are linden flowers, osmanthus, mint, and tulsi.

Minty Sencha Blend

Iced or hot mint sencha blend is perfect for all seasons, and you can also add spearmint leaves if you wish. If you choose to make it as an iced tea, you can add some cucumber. To make this blend, simply mix together:

* Chinese Sencha Green (two tablespoons)
* Dried mint and dried lemongrass (a teaspoon each)

WHITE TEA

White tea has antioxidant properties, help the body's response to inflammation, and supports brain health. It also benefits your dental health because it contains fluoride, catechins, and tannins.

Originally from China, white tea is incredibly high in antioxidants and lower in caffeine than most tea types. Its flavor is usually softer, creamier, and sweeter than green tea. It may taste fruity, floral, nutty, or even slightly vegetal.

White tea is the more delicate one to pair with; it blends well with citruses, sage, violet leaf, palmarosa, orange blossom, and fresh mint. For example, White Peony, a fresh floral bouquet with a bright finish, pairs well with comforting elements like lavender and jasmine-scented green tea.

Earl Gray Blend

Early Gray is a classic white blend, which can be spiced up with flowers. However, you should be careful not to add too many flowers, as they can easily ruin the taste. To make it, you can combine:

* Earl Gray (two tablespoons)
* Lavender or rose petals (a pinch)

White Spice Blend

This blend is both spicy and sweet, while it also contains caffeine. To make this blend, you'll need to combine:

* Pai Mu Tan (two tablespoons)
* Dried strawberries (a teaspoon)
* Peppercorns (half a teaspoon) and safflower (a pinch)

HERBAL TEA

While herbal tea or infusion is packaged like tea, infused like tea, and enjoyed like tea, it does not contain any tea leaves.

Herbal tea does not share the elaborated processing techniques that give tea its unique characteristics; it is simply the combination of boiling water and botanicals like fruits, flowers, barks, herbs, mints, spices, roots, berries and seeds. Think lavender, peppermint, orange, camomile flowers, ginger, and so on. Herbal teas are caffeine free, except for yerba mate and guayusa. They are naturally caffeinated leaves from South America, characterized by a unique balance of caffeine and a smooth, energizing effect. Guayusa has a rich, earthy, naturally smooth taste and a slightly sweet finish, while yerba mate is herbaceous and grassy with a bittersweet flavor.

Herbal teas were consumed as medicine by our ancestors. In fact, many popular blends were originally made for medicinal purposes; you probably already know the common types like chamomile, mint, and rose hip. There's no magic formula for creating the perfect blend. Simple choose the ingredients you like and blend them in the strength you like. But here are a few examples to get you started.

Hibiscus Tea

Hibiscus tea has antibacterial properties and will lower blood pressure, due to the vitamin C it contains. It can be combined with rose, lemon, cranberry, raspberry, peppermint, orange, rose hip, and apple and can be used for calming. To make a tea, combine two parts of hibiscus as the basic ingredient with half a part rosehip as the complementary ingredient, and one part rose as your supportive ingredient, or one part hibiscus with half part of peppermint as the supportive ingredient.

Hibiscus Blend

Hot or iced hibiscus blend is very refreshing and includes:
* Dried hibiscus (two tablespoons)
* Mint leaves and lemongrass (a teaspoon each)

Lemon Balm

Lemon balm can have a relaxing effect and treats indigestion, insomnia, and anxiety, while it'll also enhance your mood. It can be combined with fennel seed, peppermint, mate, linden, rose hip, calendula, and chamomile. To make a tea, you can combine one part lemon balm as your basic ingredient with one fourth part chamomile and one fourth part fennel seed as your complementary ingredients, and one part calendula as your supportive ingredient.

Chamomile

Chamomile can help with sleeping problems, stomach problems, and anxiety, since it helps you relax and doesn't have caffeine. Generally, it mixes well with white and green tea. The ingredients for this blend are:
* Dried chamomile (two tablespoons).
* Dried ginger root (a teaspoon). If you're using it for sleep problems, you can replace the ginger with valerian root, to make it stronger.
* Dried licorice root (half a teaspoon).

Rooibos

Rooibos helps you relax and calms the central nervous system, because it doesn't contain any caffeine. It's perfect for nighttime, as it'll help you sleep easier, especially if you're suffering from insomnia. It can be combined with cinnamon, orange, carob, dried strawberry, rose, lavender, and vanilla. To make a tea, you can combine one part of it as your basic ingredient with one part orange zest and one part dried strawberries as your supportive ingredients, or one part of it with one pinch of lavender as the complementary ingredient and one pinch of vanilla as the supportive ingredient.

Apple Herbal Blend

Since rooibos is the base, this herbal tea is very sweet and has no caffeine, which makes it suitable for children too. The ingredients for this blend are:

* Rooibos tea (two tablespoons)
* A cinnamon stick of about one inch
* Dried apple (one or two teaspoons)
* A vanilla pod of about half an inch

Herbal Chocolate Blend

To make this blend, put a teaspoon of chocolate drops in a small pan that is placed on top of a larger pan, where water is boiling. Then, combine:

* Pure Rooibos tea (two tablespoons)
* A vanilla pod of about one inch and cocoa shells (half a teaspoon)

Other Tea Ingredients, Properties & Recipes

Peppermint is great to ease tension and cool a sore throat, as it has antibacterial properties.

~

Ginger will warm you up and combat nausea and has the magical properties of love, success, and power. Add the magical properties of lemon for a double cup of love but also friendship, purification, and the power of the moon. Truly simple: use a few slices of ginger and a squeeze of lemon.

~

Rose hip contains a lot of vitamin C and goes well with lemongrass, chamomile or green tea.

~

Yerba Mate will treat indigestion and boost your metabolism because it has a lot of caffeine.

~

Osmanthus, lemongrass, and lavender mix well with white tea.

~

Calendula will treat colds, period cramps, fever, stomach problems, gum problems, and will stimulate blood pressure, due to its antibiotic, anti-inflammatory, and astringent properties.

~

Berries are great in light herbal tea. I would avoid adding them in green or black tea.

~

Fennel seeds are used for various digestive problems and half. Adding half a teaspoon per cup brings you healing, purification, and protection. Fennel and chamomile are a great combo with a light taste and calming effects.

~

Rose petals can be used in teas; make sure to wash them first, as those in bouquets usually contain pesticide. Beside bringing love, psychic powers, luck, protection and healing, rose is an antioxidant, high in vitamin C, that is useful for fatigue, menstrual cramps, and tension. Its petals mix well with black and oolong tea. Try rose, caramel, and a hint of cherry for a seriously romantic tea.

~

Try green tea and roasted popped rice for a smooth and strong tea with powerful aromas.

~

Jasmine and green tea work well for a light floral cup.

~

Blend roasted mate, black tea, chopped ginger, cardamom, coriander, cinnamon, cloves, and black pepper for an exotic cup with lots of caffeine.

~

Tulsi mixes well with green and black tea.

~

Yellow tea is the rarest type of tea. Its taste is mild, somewhere between white and green tea.

~

Earl Gray tea with dried citrus.

Magical Tea Blends

As I said before, different teas and herbs also have magical properties. In this section, I'll share with you some tea and potion recipes that I have created while working on new intentions. You can use them to make teas to drink, adjust them to your practice, or use them in offerings and spell work.

LOVE BLENDS

You can drink these blends to help you attract love, and you can also use them in other rituals and love spells.

* Use black tea and add rose and cocoa husk.
* Use chamomile and add rose and lavender or just vanilla.
* Use hibiscus and add either vanilla or a combination of rose hip, licorice, apple, raspberry, and orange.
* You can add dried strawberry and apple in equal parts and pour in a few drops of lemon juice.
* Add dried sweet plums and figs in equal parts, along with some cinnamon and ginger.
* Mix green tea with jasmine or rose and orange.
* Mix dried raspberry with pomegranate.

GROUNDING BLENDS

The following blends can help you ground and center yourself before a ritual, as they don't contain caffeine. They'll also help you balance your energy.

* Add a little lemon, green tea, or sage to your chamomile.
* Add peppermint and licorice roots to your lemon balm.
* Mix ginger with clove.
* Combine dandelion with rose and peppermint with gin.
* Use sage in rooibos tea.

HAPPINESS BLENDS

The following blends can be used to attract joy and as part of spells and rituals.

* Combine dried rose with lemon.
* Mix mint with ginger, pomegranate, and dried raspberry.
* Add dried berries and rose to your red tea.

- Mix dried apricot with almond.
- Add dried blackberries and raspberries to your black tea.
- Mix lemon with orange and ginger.
- Add dried apple and ginger to your lemongrass.
- Add dried apple and citrus to the rosehip.
- Mix rosehip, blueberry, and sage or dried apple, cherry, and licorice with your hibiscus.
- Mix dried kiwi with lime and ginger.
- Add vanilla, pear, and ginger to lemongrass.

Chakra Healing

     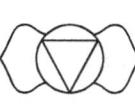 

Chakras and chakra healing have gained popularity over the recent years. Mantras help activate and balance your chakras and they're short, sacred phrases, often used repetitively in meditation to help keep you focused and grounded. Therefore, combining tea meditation and mantras for chakra healing is a good way to create a blend of different ancient practices. In this section I'll outline the different teas and blends that can help you balance your chakras.

~

MULADHARA (ROOT CHAKRA)
* **Location**: Base of the spine
* **Emotions**: Security and safety
* **Color**: Red
* **Mantra**: 'I am'
* **Herbs**: Cinnamon bark, dandelion root, elderflower, sage, ginger, and hibiscus
* **Tea suggestion**: Ginger tea

SVADHISTHANA (SACRAL CHAKRA)
* **Location**: Pubic bone
* **Emotions**: Flow, creativity, and pleasure
* **Color**: Orange
* **Mantra**: 'I feel'
* **Herbs**: Calendula, fennel seed, and hibiscus
* **Tea suggestion**: Calendula tea

MANIPURA (SOLAR PLEXUS CHAKRA)
* **Location**: Diaphragm
* **Emotions**: Decisiveness and wisdom of personal power
* **Color**: Yellow
* **Mantra**: 'I do'
* **Herbs**: Cinnamon, fennel, rosemary, turmeric, ginger, and marshmallow
* **Tea suggestion**: Rosemary tea

ANAHATA (HEART CHAKRA)

* **Location:** Heart
* **Emotions:** Forgiveness, love, and compassion
* **Color:** Green
* **Mantra:** 'I love'
* **Herbs:** Rose petals, hawthorn berries, and jasmine
* **Tea suggestion:** Jasmine green tea

VISHUDDHA (THROAT CHAKRA)

* **Location:** Throat
* **Emotions:** Truth, kindness, and love
* **Color:** Blue
* **Mantra:** 'I speak'
* **Herbs:** Eucalyptus, lemon balm, red clover flowers, peppermint leaf, and sage
* **Tea suggestion:** Red clover tea

AJNA (THIRD EYE CHAKRA)

* **Location:** Between the eyebrows
* **Emotions:** Intuition, sensitivity, and openness to inner perception
* **Color:** Indigo
* **Mantra:** 'I see'
* **Herbs:** Jasmine, lemon, mint, rosemary leaf, and eyebright
* **Tea suggestion:** Mint tea

SAHASRARA (CROWN CHAKRA)

* **Location:** Top of the head
* **Emotions:** Enlightenment, wisdom, connection to the Source, and awareness
* **Color:** Purple
* **Mantra:** 'I understand'
* **Herbs:** Lotus root, lavender, tulsi leaf, and Gotu Kola
* **Tea suggestion:** Lavender tea

Zodiac Blends

Tea can also be used, according to your sign, to enhance your positive characteristics and ease the negatives. Astrology blends can also be incorporated into rituals that have to do with seasons. Let's say, for example, you want to use the Aries blend for a ritual corresponding to the Sun entering Aries or the Virgo blend for a ceremony when the Moon is entering Virgo. Here you'll find a blend recipe for each sign.

~

CAPRICORN (DECEMBER 22–JANUARY 19)

- **Element:** Earth
- **Ruling planet:** Saturn
- **House:** 10th house of social status
- **Blend:** A bitter, fresh, strong, and deep blend, which will boost your confidence to achieve your goals, is the perfect flavor combination if you're a Capricorn, because you often need to relax and unwind from all of your responsibilities.
- **Herbs and plants:** Nutmeg, roasted chicory, marshmallow root, alfalfa, and assam.

SAGITTARIUS (NOVEMBER 22–DECEMBER 21)

- **Element:** Fire
- **Ruling planet:** Jupiter
- **House:** 9th house of wisdom and philosophy
- **Blend:** A chocolate, earthy, deep, cinnamon, and spicy blend is the most suitable combination if you're a Sagittarius, as it'll help your enthusiastic and adventure-seeking nature.
- **Herbs and plants:** Ginger, cacao, eleuthero, dandelion root, cinnamon, and assam.

SCORPIO (OCTOBER 23–NOVEMBER 21)

* **Element**: Water
* **Ruling planets**: Pluto and Mars
* **House**: 8th house of bonding, mystery, transformation, sex, death, and birth.
* **Blend**: An earthy, aromatic, lavender, sweet, herbal, and light blend is the perfect herbal combination if you're a Scorpio, as it'll help you let go of the need to control.
* **Herbs and plants**: Lavender, sweet woodruff, shatavari, raspberry leaf, and assam.

LIBRA (SEPTEMBER 23–OCTOBER 22)

* **Element**: Air
* **Ruling planet**: Venus
* **House**: 7th house of partnership
* **Blend**: An earthy, dark, herbal, citrus, and deep blend that will keep you motivated is the perfect flavor combination if you're a Libra.
* **Herbs and plants**: Slippery elm, plantain leaf, milk thistle, eleuthero, roasted chicory, red rooibos, orange peel, and assam.

VIRGO (AUGUST 23–SEPTEMBER 22)

* **Element**: Earth
* **Ruling planet**: Mercury
* **House**: 6th house of service, lineage, and legacy
* **Blend**: An intensive, herbal, refreshing, spicy, and minty blend, which will help ground, soothe, and refresh you, is the ideal flavor combination if you're a Virgo.
* **Herbs and plants**: Clove, peppermint, fenugreek, and assam.

LEO (JULY 23–AUGUST 22)

* **Element**: Fire
* **Ruling planet**: Sun
* **House**: 5th house of pleasure
* **Blend**: A vibrant, refreshing, citrus, herbal, and light blend that will help you harness your charisma and sociability is the perfect flavor combination for Leo.
* **Herbs and plants**: Lotus leaf, lemongrass, hawthorn berries, and assam.

CANCER (JUNE 21–JULY 22)

* **Element**: Water
* **Ruling planet**: Moon
* **House**: 4th house of home and family
* **Blend**: A strong, dark, spicy, fruity, slightly bitter, and deep blend is the most suitable combination if you're a Cancer, because it will deepen your intuition and help you care for yourself or others.
* **Herbs and plants**: Roasted chicory, strawberry leaf, cardamom, orange peel, and assam.

GEMINI (MAY 21–JUNE 20)

* **Element:** Air
* **Ruling planet:** Mercury
* **House:** 3rd house of sharing
* **Blend:** A lively, refreshing, ginger, minty, herbal, and light tea blend is the perfect combination if you're a Gemini, because it'll help you tap into your imagination and cheerfulness.
* **Herbs and plants:** Spearmint, red clover leaf, ginger root, allspice, and assam.

TAURUS (APRIL 20–MAY 20)

* **Element:** Earth
* **Ruling planet:** Venus
* **House:** 2nd house of value
* **Blend:** An earthy, mellow, mild, herbal, and light tea blend is the perfect combination if you're a Taurus, because it will help you connect to the earth.
* **Herbs and plants:** Wild pau d'arco, calendula flowers, blackberry leaf, and assam.

ARIES (MARCH 21–APRIL 19)

* **Element:** Fire
* **Ruling planet:** Mars
* **House:** 1st house of the self
* **Blend:** A green, mellow, herbal, mild, and light blend, which will give you a new perspective and mental clarity, is the most suitable flavor combination if you're an Aries.
* **Herbs and plants:** Sage, amla, periwinkle, lemon balm, holy basil, chrysanthemum flowers, and assam.

PISCES (FEBRUARY 19–MARCH 20)

* **Element:** Water
* **Ruling planets:** Neptune and Jupiter
* **House:** 12th house of sacrifice
* **Blend:** An aromatic, deep, apple, fruity, spicy, and cinnamon blend is the perfect flavor combination if you're a Pisces, as it will help you when you're feeling exposed or vulnerable.
* **Herbs and plants:** Rosehip, echinacea, cinnamon, and assam.

AQUARIUS (JANUARY 20–FEBRUARY 18)

* **Element:** Air
* **Ruling planets:** Uranus and Saturn
* **House:** 11th house of blessings
* **Blend:** A slightly fruity, mild, slightly sweet, herbal, and light blend that will help you expand your mind and focus is the ideal flavor combination if you're an Aquarius.
* **Herbs and plants:** Maqui berry, chickweed, butcher's broom, violet, red rooibos, and assam.

Part 2

Potions & Brews

"Tea ... is a religion of the art of life."
— Kakuzō Okakura, The Book of Tea

Moonbrews

In many ancient cultures, the Moon Goddess was a central figure. Considering that the menstrual cycle (about 28 days) is the same as the cycle of the moon (29.5 days), the moon has been associated with the Divine Feminine. Today, the moon and Moon Goddesses are still worshiped. As such, Moon tea is a cold brew that involves leaving the tea in the moonlight. Depending on the desired result, the herbs themselves or the potion can be left under the light of the Moon in different phases. For example, when the Moon is full, it represents clarity, realization of desires, power, and completion. Having said that, in this section I'm going to discuss Moon tea recipes for honoring the Goddess.

~

Blue Moon Tea

The blue moon occurs once in every four full moons of each season, and sometimes appears blue. It's particularly potent and powerful, so it's useful for rituals and spells. To make this herbal tea, you'll need:

* Chamomile flowers (four tablespoons)
* Cornflower petals (half a cup)
* Lavender buds (half a cup)
* Earl Gray loose leaf (a cup)

Lightly stir the ingredients to mix them. Add a tablespoon of the mixture to every cup of water you're boiling. Let it steep for three to five minutes. If you prefer it sweeter, add some sugar.

Honoring the Divine Feminine

This full moon tea is suitable for honoring the Goddess or the Divine Feminine and should be made when the moon is full. You don't need to leave the brew outside. A window, where the moonlight shines, works just as well. For this tea you'll need:

* Mint
* Cramp bark
* Blessed thistle
* Motherwort
* Lemon balm
* Muslin

Put two tablespoons of each herb in the muslin and tie it like a bag. Fill a mason jar with four cups of water and put the muslin bag in so that it floats. Then, leave it under the moonlight and collect it before the sun comes up. Store it indoors in a cool place.

Full Moon Tea for Intuition & Grounding

You can drink full moon tea before rituals, as it grounds you, gives you energy, and heightens your intuition. The herbs you're going to use are:

* Lemon zest from one fourth of a lemon
* Hibiscus petals (half a tablespoon)
* Rose petals (a tablespoon)
* Chamomile flowers (a tablespoon)

Put all the ingredients in a mason jar and place it somewhere where the Moon is shining. Collect before sunlight.

Lavender Moon Milk

Lavender milk tea is ideal for the nighttime and will help you sleep better, since it relaxes you. To make it, you'll need the following:

* A few blueberries
* Honey (a tablespoon)
* Chamomile (half a tablespoon)
* Lavender (a tablespoon)
* Any type of milk (a cup)

Warm up the milk and add all the ingredients. Enjoy it warm.

New Moon Tea

The new moon is the time to perform a spell/ritual related to accepting new opportunities, harnessing inner wisdom, breaking away from harmful thoughts, and positive changes. For this tea, you'll need to mix equal parts of:

* Lemon peel
* Oat straw
* Catnip
* Lemon balm
* Lavender, chamomile, and calendula flowers
* Skullcap
* Red clover

Add four tablespoons of the mix to a mason jar. Fill it with boiling water, let it steep for a couple of minutes, strain, and drink. If you wish, you can leave the herbs outside to be charged by the moon.

Waxing Moon Tea

The waxing moon is associated with success, power, excitement, luck, and abundance and is ideal for adding power to an intention that was set during the new moon. For this tea, lightly mix the following ingredients:

* Five star anise
* Cardamom pods (two tablespoons)
* Pink peppercorns (two tablespoons)
* Whole clove (two tablespoons)
* Cinnamon chips (four tablespoons)
* Red clover blossoms (half a cup)
* Darjeeling loose leaves (a cup)

Put the mixture in a mason jar. Then, put a tablespoon of it in a tea bag or strainer and brew for two to three minutes.

Emotional Healing

Blockage Remover

This recipe will remove emotional or psychological blockages and the ingredients are:

* Rosemary
* Ginger
* Lemon juice

Mix the ingredients in equal parts and pour boiling water over them. Let the mixture steep for five minutes, strain, and put it in a glass jar. Tie a pink ribbon around the jar and leave it next to a rose quartz crystal to charge.

Broken Heart Sun Tea

It's best that you make this tea on a Sunday for maximum results. You're going to need:

* A little honey
* Dried mint
* Orange peel
* Dried chamomile
* Dried rose petals
* Green tea

Start by mixing the green tea, rose, chamomile, orange peel, and mint. Then, fill a large jar with water and add two tablespoons of the mixed herbs. Let it steep in the sun for four to five hours. Strain, add the honey, and drink hot or cold.

Tea for Emotional Exhaustion

This tea will bring you self-love and comfort for when you're feeling emotionally exhausted. You'll need:

* A little honey
* Any type of milk
* Cinnamon
* Vanilla black tea

Pour hot milk over the tea bag and add some cinnamon. Then, add some honey and stir clockwise (if you want to bring comfort) or counterclockwise (to banish negativity). Place quartz and amethyst next to your mug to charge it.

Positiviteas

Confidence Boost

A confidence potion will help you connect with your masculine energy, especially if you're experiencing gender dysphoria. To make it, you'll need:

* Juniper
* Ginger
* Basil

Combine the herbs, pour boiling water over them, and stir clockwise. You can add honey or any other sweetener of your choice, if you wish.

Hard Day Potion

This potion is suitable for when you're having a hard day and need to regain positivity and energy. To make it, you only need:

* Cinnamon
* Lemon balm
* Black tea

Simply brew the black tea and add the lemon balm, stirring clockwise. Then, add the cinnamon and stir clockwise again, focusing your mind on releasing the negativity.

Happiness Potion

This recipe is designed to make you feel happier and more relaxed, as well as to expel stress and sadness. To make it, you'll need:

* Any type of milk
* A little honey or agave
* Yarrow flower
* Lemongrass
* Chamomile
* Lavender

Combine the herbs and brew for five minutes. Add honey or agave and milk, and stir clockwise.

Honey Milk Tea

Honey milk tea is a very easy happiness tea recipe that will instantly bring you positivity. You'll need:

* Milk (half a cup)
* Cinnamon (half a teaspoon)
* Honey (two teaspoons)

Boil half a cup of water and mix it with the honey and the cinnamon. Then, froth the milk and add it to the tea. Place clear quartz and citrine next to your cup to boost your optimism. If you want, you can stir a sigil in your tea for more positivity.

Hope Brew

A hope potion will make you feel more security and a slight uplift on the days you need it the most. You can drink it either hot or cold, using the following:

* A little honey
* Lemon peel or zest
* Thyme
* Black tea
* Blueberries

Simply combine all the ingredients, steep for five minutes, strain, and drink.

Positive Thoughts

A tea for positive thoughts will relax and uplift you when you're having a rough day, week, year, or lifetime. You're going to need:

* A little honey
* A sliced strawberry
* A few blueberries
* A slice of orange
* Black tea

Pour boiling water over the black tea and let it steep for five minutes. Then, add the rest of the ingredients, let it steep for another five minutes, strain, and drink.

Summer Joy Tea

Perfect for a day under the sun, this tea will give you happiness, positivity, and love. The ingredients are:

- * Strawberry
- * Rose hip
- * Apple
- * Orange peel
- * Lemongrass
- * Chamomile

Simply brew the chamomile for five minutes, add the rest of the ingredients, and let it cool down. Strain and enjoy.

Courage

This blend will give you the strength and the courage you need on days when you're feeling low. To make it, you'll need:

- * Ceylon black tea
- * Vanilla green tea
- * Grapefruit extract
- * Marigold flowers

Simply pour boiling water over the blend and let it steep for three minutes. Afterwards, strain and drink.

Good Fortune

This fortune blend contains many red fruits, because red is associated with good luck and abundance. To make it, the ingredients include:

- * Loose leaf Pu-erh tea
- * Cornflower petals
- * Pomegranate
- * Blueberry
- * Strawberry
- * Raspberry

Lightly mix all your ingredients and use one or two teaspoons of the blend per cup of tea.

Joy & Inner Peace

A tea for joy gives you a boost and increases a sense of inner peace. Use the following ingredients to make it:

* Lemon juice
* Honey
* Chamomile or sideritis

After you have brewed the tea, add the lemon and the honey. Stir clockwise and chant.

Uplifting Tea

An uplifting tea will give you more energy and positivity. You can combine the herbs by stirring clockwise, using a mortar and pestle. This blend can also be added to your bath or you can drink it as a cold brew. To make it, mix in equal parts:

* Lemongrass
* Lavender
* Mint
* Lemon balm
* Chamomile

Simply pour boiling water over the ingredients and let the tea steep for about five minutes. Then, strain and enjoy.

Truth Tea

This blend is to speak and hear the truth, no matter what. Share the tea with whoever you need to hear and share the truth. If the person you need the truth from will not drink the tea with you, submerge their name in a separate glass of the tea while you drink yours. To make this tea, you will need:

* Peppermint
* Ginger
* Lemongrass

Sweeten with honey or sugar if you wish to add a hit of love. Pray, "*Show me the truth, tell me the truth, let everyone who drinks this tea speak the truth.*"

Self–Love Potions

Love Yourself Herbal Blend

Most people in modern society have been taught that they aren't good, beautiful, or smart enough. Therefore, there's an overall lack of self-love and a tendency to forget about ourselves and our needs. This tea will help you prioritize yourself, and it's useful to have this blend at hand before self-love rituals or spells. You're going to need the following ingredients:

* Dried rose petals (a pinch)
* Cardamom pods (about five)
* Fennel seeds (half a teaspoon)
* Chopped licorice root (a teaspoon)

Crush the licorice root, using a mortar and pestle, along with the cardamom pods and the fennel seeds. Boil about two cups of water and add all the ingredients, apart from the rose petals. Let it boil for about 10 minutes and add the rose petals right before you serve it.

Warm Your Spirit

This is another self-love tea that will bring you positivity and love. You'll need:

* A little honey (preferably lavender honey)
* Jasmine (half a teaspoon)
* Chamomile (half a teaspoon)
* Dried mango (half a teaspoon)
* Lemon peel
* Orange peel
* Rose hip (a teaspoon)
* Hibiscus (two teaspoons)

Bring some water to a boil and pour over the mixed ingredients. Strain, let it steep for five minutes, and add the honey, stirring clockwise.

Self-Love Iced Tea

This is a very refreshing drink for warm summer days that will boost your confidence and self-love. For the iced tea, you'll need:

* White sugar (a tablespoon)
* Any light tea (a cup)
* Mint leaves (about eight)
* Raspberries (about five)

Mix the sugar, mint, and a tablespoon of the tea, using a mortar and pestle. Then, strain the mixture and put it in another bowl. After that, place the raspberries inside and squeeze them to get the juice out. Strain and place the juice in a cup, where you'll add the rest of the tea, some mint leaves, and ice.

Self-Love Booster

Self-love tea promotes healing, love, protection, and attraction and banishes negativity when you're feeling down or need a boost of self-love. To make it, you'll need:

* A little honey
* Chamomile (half a teaspoon)
* Dandelion root or black tea (half a teaspoon)
* Whole cloves (a third of a teaspoon)
* Basil (half a teaspoon)
* Dried rose petals (a teaspoon)

After you've mixed the ingredients, pour hot water over them, and let the tea steep for about four or five minutes. Then, strain and drink.

Inner Voice & Intuition

This self-love tea may help you learn to listen to your inner self and give your intuition the space and freedom to come through.

* Dried rose petals (a tablespoon)
* Hibiscus petals (a tablespoon)
* Coconut butter (a tablespoon)
* Ground cinnamon (half a teaspoon)
* Honey (half a teaspoon)
* A pinch of cardamom

Steep the dried hibiscus and rose petals for about 10 minutes. Then strain and blend with the coconut butter, cinnamon, cardamom, and honey. Sip your cup while sitting in front of a mirror and writing a love letter to yourself.

Self-Love & Empowerment Tea Spell

Sometimes we all need to remind ourselves that we are beautiful, spiritual beings.

WHAT YOU NEED:

* Rose petals (a teaspoon) for love, protection and healing
* Fresh or dry jasmine flowers (half a teaspoon) for love, dreams and divination
* Ground cinnamon (a quater teaspoon) for spirituality, success, healing, shielding and love
* A pinch of ground clove for protection and love
* Honey (a tablespoon)
* Almond or coconut milk (a cup)
* A clear quartz, rose quartz, or amethyst crystal (or all three)

WHAT'S NEXT:

1. In a small pot, heat some water. Lower the heat to medium and add rose petals and jasmine flowers.
2. After steeping for about 3-5 minutes, add milk, clove, and cinnamon.
3. Then, add the honey, and turn the heat off.
4. Stir gently, and then pour into your cup.
5. Hold the crystal in the receiving hand (your left hand) and observe the steam that rises off the cup while you visualize it as golden wisps of light radiating from your cup. Acknowledge how calm and content you feel and remind yourself that you deserve this peace.
6. Switch the crystal to the giving hand (your right hand). Recite each line of the following chant in your mind as you sip with the crystal in your right hand and your cup still in your left.

> *"I am blessed and deserving,*
> *I know that I am worthy,*
> *From honey and milk, a heart as gentle as silk,*
> *From sky and water, a strength that never falters,*
> *From rosebuds and thorns, a beauty that can't be worn,*
> *From salt and earth, this is my rebirth,*
> *For I know now I am worthy,*
> *Energy and love flow like milk and honey*
> *And so it is."*

7. To amplify the benefits, place the crystals under your pillow when you sleep. Remember to cleanse and charge them the following morning.

Energy Healing

Calming Tea Blend

This calming tea blend can reduce anxiety and stress. To make it, you're going to need:

* Honey
* Lemon juice
* White tea (a teaspoon)
* Turmeric (a pinch)
* Lemon balm (half a teaspoon)
* Lavender (half a teaspoon)
* Chamomile (half a teaspoon)

Place the chamomile, lavender, lemon balm, turmeric, and white tea in a teabag. Warm up two cups of water, pour it over the teabag, and let it steep for three or four minutes. Add the honey and lemon and enjoy.

Grounding Citrus Tea

A grounding tea can offer the relaxation and determination you need to ground yourself. The ingredients you'll need are:

* Chestnut
* Clove
* Dandelion
* Cardamom
* Mint
* Chamomile
* Lemon slices or juice
* Orange slices or juice

Brew the chamomile and stir clockwise. Then, add the orange and the lemon and infuse for a few minutes. After that, add the herbs and stir clockwise. Finally, add the clove and the chestnut while chanting.

Healing Matcha

This is a great blend if you need a boost during a period when you're going through a lot. To make this tea, you're going to need:

* Matcha
* Rose
* Lavender

Pour boiling water over the mixture of rose and lavender and leave it for a few minutes. Place a scoop of matcha in another bowl, strain the floral tea, and pour it over the matcha. Then, stir clockwise and imagine your body filling with positive energy.

Higher Self Tea Blend

A higher self tea can help you strengthen the connection between spirit, mind, and body, due to its relaxing properties and balanced yin and yang energies. For this blend, mix in equal parts:

* Holy Basil
* Gotu Kola
* Cardamom
* Shatavari
* Ashwagandha
* Jasmine
* Rose petals

Banishing Negativity & Gaining Courage

This tea is designed to drink in the morning during Fall or a rainy day, but feel free to use it as you please. For this tea, you're going to need:

* A little honey or sugar
* Nutmeg and cinnamon (a teaspoon each)
* Milk
* Black spiced Chai

Put the black spiced Chai on a tea bag and place it in a mug. Pour boiling water over it and let it steep for five minutes. Then, add milk, cinnamon, nutmeg, and honey or sugar if you like.

Centering

For this recipe you will be using holy basil as your basic ingredient. However, don't consume this tea if you're pregnant or trying to conceive (this applies to men too). This tea helps you relax and clear your mind, so it's perfect for those times when you're feeling very stressed. To make this tea, you're going to need:

- Honey (a tablespoon)
- Dry hibiscus (a tablespoon)
- A slice of ginger
- Dried holy basil (two and a half tablespoons)

Place the holy basil and the hibiscus in a strainer and pour boiling water over it in a clockwise motion. Then, add the ginger and let it steep for five minutes. Remove the strainer, add the honey, and stir counterclockwise, while chanting.

Cleansing

If you want to meditate or do yoga, you can start with this tea. To make it, you'll need the following:

- Mint
- Sage
- Green or white tea

Brew the tea for five minutes, stirring clockwise, strain, and drink.

Yogi Tea

This tea will make you feel warmed up and cleansed, while it'll also give you energy. The ingredients include:

- A little coconut milk
- Some fennel seeds
- Cloves (three or four)
- A cinnamon stick
- Black peppercorns (four to six)
- Cardamom pods (four to six)
- Ginger (an inch)

Start by thinly slicing the ginger and cracking the cardamom pods. Then, lightly mix the ingredients along with four cups of water, cover, and simmer for an hour on low heat. After that, strain, add the coconut milk, and serve.

Releasing Negativity Tea Spell

This tea spell can give you some new perspective, it will help you see the negative impact that energy has had in and on your body, and it will permit you to process it.

I would suggest you perform this spell during a storm.

WHAT YOU NEED:

* Storm water (alternatively, moon water is fine)
* Rosemary for protection, love, purification, and healing
* Lavender for peace, protection, happiness and purification
* Chamomile for calming, love and purifications
* Peppermint for purification, love, healing and psychic powers
* Amethyst crystal for calming
* Paper and pen

WHAT'S NEXT:

1. Whisper your intentions into the empty mug
2. Add the ingredients to the infuser and steep in hot storm/moon water for 5 minutes.

Stir counter-clockwise, close your eyes, and, while visualizing the negative energy leaving your body, chant:

> *"Like a storm passes on over strong winds*
> *My life's dark storms move on*
> *And I am free to the clearest skies*
> *And the sun's shining blessings."*
> *Repeat as many times as you would like.*

3. Write on a piece of paper everything that has been troubling you lately.
4. Rip the paper away from you while visualizing yourself, filling with light energy and releasing all stress in your body. Breathe deeply
5. Burn the scraps of paper in a cauldron or bowl and bury the ashes outside
6. Enjoy your tea! Watch the rain while drinking it and smile!

Nighttime

Maiden Tea

This maiden tea has a relaxing effect, so it's ideal for nighttime. It will also give you perfect glowing skin and healthy hair. You're going to need:

- A little honey or sugar
- Lemon juice
- Coconut oil (a teaspoon)
- Two slices of lemon
- Chamomile flowers (half a teaspoon)
- Hibiscus flowers (a teaspoon)
- Spearmint (half a teaspoon)
- Green tea (a teaspoon)

Warm up three cups of water, but don't boil it. Combine the green tea, spearmint, hibiscus, chamomile, and lemon. Pour the hot water over the mixture, add the lemon and sugar or honey and enjoy.

Sleep Potion

A sleep potion will help you if you're having trouble sleeping and will instantly relax you. To make it, you'll need:

- One star anise
- Nutmeg (a pinch)
- A cinnamon stick
- St. John's Wort (half a teaspoon)
- Chamomile (half a teaspoon)
- Lavender (half a teaspoon)

Mix all the ingredients lightly and add boiling water. Let it steep for 15 minutes and add warm milk. Don't drink this tea if you're on common medications or antidepressants, as St. John's Wort is known to counteract them.

Sweet Dreams

A sweet dreams tea is useful for insomnia, and to make this tea, you're going to lightly mix:

- Spearmint (half a tablespoon)
- Valerian root (a tablespoon)
- Catnip (a tablespoon)
- Chamomile (a tablespoon)
- Lemon Balm (two tablespoons)

Simply pour boiling water over the mix and let it steep for about 15 minutes. If you're having a very hard time sleeping, you can add half a tablespoon of Valerian root more.

Milk Tea for Better Sleep

Milk tea is known for its calming properties and is especially helpful for when you're having trouble sleeping. To make it, you'll need:

- Vanilla extract
- Thyme (a teaspoon)
- Chamomile (two teaspoons)
- White rose (two teaspoons)
- Lavender (a teaspoon)

Simply mix all the ingredients and pour boiling water over them. Let the tea steep for five minutes, strain, add the vanilla extract, and drink.

Dream Potion

This blend weaves together the magic of these six herbs. It can help calm the nervous system, boost your mood, and connect you deeply to your cosmic center. To make it, ass equal parts of the following ingredients:

- Blue lotus
- Damiana
- Mugwort
- Hibiscus
- Raspberry leaf
- Marshmallow leaf

Use one heaped teaspoon in your tea strainer and let it steep for 7 minutes before drinking—beautiful mixed with some honey.

Everyday Potions

Afternoon Energizing Blend

An energizing blend will give you the energy you need after a long day. To make it, mix the following:

* Mint
* Echinacea
* Lemongrass

Pour hot water over the ingredients and let it steep for five minutes. Then, strain and drink.

Creativitea

Creativity is associated with the Svadhisthana or the sacral chakra. It is also associated with the colors orange and yellow, and with crystals like amethyst, amazonite, carnelian, lapis lazuli, celestite, and clear quartz. You can use these in your ritual as you please. For example, you can use orange or yellow candles and some of the crystals. To make a tea that enhances your creativity, you'll need the following:

* Sage
* Lemon Verbena
* Rose petals
* Lavender
* Chamomile

Lightly mix the dried herbs and use one and a half teaspoons of the mixture for every cup of tea. Pour boiling water over it while visualizing creative energy flowing over you and stir clockwise. Let it steep for three minutes, strain, and drink. If you want it to be more potent, you can use full moon water.

Empowerment Tea

An empowerment tea will give you the necessary energy and concentration to perform tasks or study. To make it, you'll need to mix:

* Cinnamon
* Sugar
* Darjeeling tea

Brew the tea for five minutes and then add the cinnamon and sugar. Let it steep for another five minutes, strain, and drink.

Gender Dysphoria

If you're struggling with gender dysphoria, this tea will give you a boost of confidence and make you feel affirmed. The basic ingredients you're going to need are:

* Honey
* Ground ginger
* Black tea leaves

The additional ingredients for feminine identities are:

* Cardamom pods
* Blackberry
* Heather

For masculine identities, use the following:

* Cloves
* Chrysanthemum petals
* Basil leaves

If your gender identity falls into a non-binary spectrum, you can use the following:

* Cinquefoil
* Geranium
* Lemongrass

Brew the tea leaves and the ginger for a few minutes and then add the herbs. After that, let the tea steep for four or five minutes. Strain and drink.

Productivitea

This is an energizing tea that will make you more productive. To make it, you'll need:

* Green tea
* Cardamom
* Rosemary
* Ginger

Brew the green tea for five minutes, then add cardamom, rosemary, and ginger in equal parts. Stir clockwise and let it steep for a few more minutes.

The Power to Succeed Tea Spell

We all need a little boost sometimes. Perhaps it's before a big test, a date or even when cooking a meal for your friends. We all want to succeed in something (neither big nor small), and the odds may not be in our favor. This tea spell will definitely boost your chances, but it does not guarantee that you will get the outcome you desire.

WHAT YOU NEED:

* Green tea for health, love and passion, energy, cleansing, and money
* Sassafras root bark for positive results
* Dandelions leaf for manifesting wishes and requests, it acts as a catalyst
* Comfrey root for bringing in money
* Ginger for success, prosperity, confidence

WHAT'S NEXT:

1. Add the ingredients to the strainer and steep in hot water for 5 minutes.
2. Strain the ingredients out if you like
3. Stir clockwise and chant:

    "Like the snowdrop that blooms in winter, I prevail.

    Like the opening of spring, give me the power to bloom.

    As the calluna buds, I rise with the sun as the breeze flows through me.

    Give me luck and success."

4. Visualize yourself pushing through something hard and entering relief. Then take your first sip.

Easy Black Tea Prosperity Spells

I love using prosperity spells because I have learned over time not to think of money as evil but as neutral. As I use the money to improve the lives of those around me, I know I am using my abundance mindset for good.

Cinnamon is very potent and attracts wealth faster than any other herb. You could even keep a small bowl of cinnamon on your altar as an offering.

WHAT YOU NEED:

* Black tea for courage, prosperity, and money
* Cinnamon for drawing wealth
* Honey, symbolically used to stick you and money together

WHAT'S NEXT:

1. Boil some water and pour it into your mug of choice. If you are using loose leaves, fill the tea cage.
2. Hold the cup between your hands and visualize a large golden coin in its place.
3. As you drop the tea bag into the water, visualize the coin splashing into the tea. Chant:

    "May wealth find me when I'm in need,"

4. Add honey and recite:

    "And may this potion bind wealth to me,"

5. Then, stir clockwise and repeat:

    "This is my will, so shall it be."

6. Breathe your energy into the tea and drink it.
7. You can envision yourself drinking liquid gold instead of black tea.

Reflective Vibe

If you want some moments of reflection, this tea can calm you, due to its relaxing properties. You're going to need:

* Lapsang Souchong
* Keemun
* Oolong

Simply pour hot water over the ingredients and let the tea steep for five minutes. You can also place your cup next to quartz, tourmaline, and lapis lazuli, to charge it with the crystals' energy.

Mental Focus

A mental focus tea will keep you inspired and motivated throughout the day and will give you the concentration and clarity you need. To make it, you'll need:

* Yellow mustard seed (a pinch)
* Lemon verbena (a pinch)
* Mint (a teaspoon)
* Rosemary (a teaspoon)

Bring a cup of water to a boil and add the ingredients. Then, let it steep for five minutes, strain, and drink.

Abundance & Money

The following herbs are known in folklore to bring abundance and money. Combining them in a tea will give you exactly that. You'll need:

* Alfalfa
* Nutmeg
* All spice
* Dried pineapple
* Coconut oolong tea

Simply mix them, pour boiling water over, let them steep for five minutes, strain, and drink.

For Change

This tea is great if you're entering any type of transition in your life and for the beginning of a new year, as it'll help you with anxiety, uncertainty, and new pressures. You'll need the following:

* A little honey
* Black pepper (a pinch)
* Lemon balm (a teaspoon)
* Honeysuckle (a teaspoon)
* Peppermint (a tablespoon)

Add the peppermint, honeysuckle, lemon balm, and black pepper in a tea bag. Put the tea bag in a cup of boiling water and leave it for three to five minutes. Stir clockwise and add the honey.

Motivation

A motivation tea is very simple and can help you get through the day, as it gives you lots of motivation. The ingredients you're going to need are:

* A little honey
* Sun water
* Ginger
* Rosemary
* Cinnamon
* Black tea

Simply mix all your ingredients with sun water and let the tea steep for five minutes. Enjoy it warm.

Relaxation

A relaxation tea will keep you refreshed and relaxed at the same time. To make it, combine:

* Apricot
* Raspberry
* Cocoa nibs
* Rooibos

Pour boiling water over the mixture and let it steep for five minutes. Then, strain and enjoy.

Ignite Your Inner Flame

An inner flame tea will give you more confidence and help you discover your inner beauty. You'll need:

* A little honey
* Dried hibiscus (two and a half tablespoons)
* Ginseng powder (one fourth of a teaspoon)
* Lemon juice from one lemon
* Cinnamon (one and a half sticks)

Bring four cups of water to a boil, turn the stove on low heat and add the cinnamon, lemon juice, ginseng, and hibiscus. Leave it for ten minutes, turn off the heat, and let it steep for another five minutes. Pour it in a mug, add the honey (if you wish), and stir clockwise while chanting.

Soothe Agitation

This is a drinkable spell you can use for getting rid of worries and calming your anxiety. You're going to need:

* A little honey
* Cinnamon
* Earl Gray or chamomile

First, brew the tea for five minutes. Then, add the honey and stir counterclockwise while visualizing the worries leaving your body. Finally, add the cinnamon and stir clockwise while imagining a calm energy surrounding you.

Meditation Herbal Tea

Drinking tea before meditation will help your body relax and your mind let go easier. The ingredients include:

* Rosehip
* Peppermint
* Fennel
* Raspberry leaf
* Dandelion
* Nettle
* Chamomile

Lightly mix your herbs and pour boiling water over them. Then, let the tea steep for five minutes, strain, and drink.

Anxiety & Stressful Situations Tea Spell

This spell can be used to destress yourself on important days or before any situation that gives you anxiety or stress. However, this is not a cure-all or replacement for any modern medicine.

WHAT YOU NEED:

* Green tea for cleansing away negative thoughts and negative thoughts
* Honey for sweetening a situation or a potentially difficult person's thought toward you
* Bay leaf
* A Marker

WHAT'S NEXT:

1. Write the phrase, "*I have power, wisdom, and courage*" onto a bay leaf.
2. Hold it between your hands and take a few moments to focus on your intention.
3. Close your eyes and imagine yourself getting through your obstacle(s) and feel the relief once your obstacle(s) is behind you.
4. Crumble the leaf up, blow the pieces into the breeze, and know that the universe has received your desire.
5. Now you can make the tea; allow the green tea bag to sit in hot water for 2-3 minutes. Once you have removed the bag, add the honey.
6. With a spoon, slowly stir the tea clockwise.
7. Close your eyes and focus on the swirling sound of the tea, the sounds the spoon makes in the cup, etc. Also, focus on the aroma of the tea.
8. Once you feel calmer, silently repeat the following chant:

    "*I have the strength, wisdom, and courage to get through (your specific stressful situation).*"

9. Repeat this phrase to yourself until it feels true, then take a sip.
10. Allow yourself to be in the moment for a few moments: focus on the taste of the tea and how it feels in your mouth, don't rush it.
11. When it feels right, take another sip. Take a few deep breaths, and repeat the previous 3 steps until the tea is gone.
12. Throughout the rest of the day, repeat the phrase when you feel stressed about a situation and remind yourself that you put the power of the Triforce into your tea and drank it into your body.

Libido & Pleasure

Aphrodisiac Herbal Tea

An aphrodisiac tea will increase your libido and help you relax, and you can also share it with your partner. For this herbal blend, you're going to need:

* Dried oat straw (a teaspoon)
* Vanilla bean pieces (one fourth of a teaspoon)
* Dried hibiscus flowers (a tablespoon)
* Dried ginger (a teaspoon)

Chop the dried ginger and combine it with the rest of the herbs. Pour two cups of boiling water over the mixture. Then, cover, let it steep for 15 minutes, strain, and serve.

Libido Tea

A libido tea will increase your sex drive and to make it, you'll need:

* Honeysuckle
* Roses
* Hibiscus
* Peppermint
* Honey or sugar

Lightly mix the herbs and pour boiling water over them. Strain and add honey or sugar. You can serve it either hot or cold.

Sexual Arousal

A libido tea will help you get aroused easier. The ingredients include:

* A little honey or sugar
* A rose hip
* A calendula flower
* Blue lotus (a teaspoon)
* Damiana (a teaspoon)

Boil one and a half cups of water and add the herbs. Let the tea steep for five minutes, then strain and drink.

Friendship & Love

Friendship Recipe

This tea will draw others close to you and help you make new friends. The ingredients are:

* Lemon zest (a pinch)
* White tea (a teaspoon)
* Jasmine (a teaspoon)
* Hibiscus (a teaspoon)

Lightly mix the ingredients and pour hot water over them. Let it steep for five minutes, strain, and drink.

Love Is in the Air Potion

A love potion will attract love into your life. To make, you'll need the following ingredients:

* Almond milk (half a cup)
* Vanilla extract (a few drops)
* Almond extract (a few drops)
* Cinnamon (a pinch)
* Honey (a teaspoon)
* Green tea (a tablespoon)

In a cup, add half a cup of boiling water, cinnamon, vanilla extract, almond extract, and honey. Then, add the tea, cover, and leave it for a few minutes. After that, remove the tea bag and add the almond milk.

Relationship Tea

It's a great idea if you and your partner enjoy this tea together, as it's designed to maximize passion. The ingredients you'll need are:

* Mead Liquor
* Honey
* Cinnamon
* Sweet orange peel
* Lavender
* Rose petals

Pour boiling water over the rose, lavender, orange, and cinnamon. Then, add a dash of liquor, let it steep for a few minutes, and add the honey. Strain and enjoy with your partner.

Romance & Passion Tea

A romance and passion potion can attract love in your life or enhance the passion between you and someone else. For this tea, you're going to need the following:

* A cinnamon stick
* Meadowsweet or oat straw
* Jasmine
* Damiana
* Orange peel
* Hibiscus flower

Simply pour boiling water over the ingredients and let the tea steep for about five minutes. If you want, you can place your mug next to rose quartz for an extra boost of love.

Faithful Lust

This tea will help you keep a lover passionate and faithful without killing the libido. Drink this cup with your other half to tie the magic to both. To make it, you will need:

* Peppermint
* Hibiscus
* Roses
* Honeysuckle
* Honey or sugar

Boil the herbs together until they form a strong tea and sweeten with honey for long-term love or sugar for sweetness. While stirring the honey or sugar, silently chant, *"Name, keep yourself to myself"* three times.

Cold Brews

Calendula Brew

This calendula brew will give you perfect skin, but you should avoid it if you're pregnant. For this recipe, you'll only need four cups of fresh calendula flowers. To make it, simply bring four cups of water to a boil and pour it over the flowers. Let it steep for several hours, strain, and drink.

Peach Iced Tea

A peach iced beverage incorporates peach simple syrup and iced tea. You can use the peach simple syrup for other brews too, if you're a fan of peach. To make this tea, you'll need:

* Tea of your choice (four tea bags). Yellow tea and black tea go very well with peach.
* Peaches (two or three ripe ones)
* Sugar (a cup)

Start off by making the peach syrup. Thinly slice the peaches and combine them with a cup of water and the sugar. Boil the ingredients and leave them on low heat for 15 to 20 minutes. Press the peaches occasionally to break them up. Then, it's time to brew the tea by boiling eight cups of water, adding the tea bags, and leaving it for three to five minutes. After that, remove the tea bags and store in the refrigerator until it cools down. To serve, use a pitcher to combine the iced tea and peach syrup.

Iced Love Potion

What makes this love potion magical is the hibiscus, which is known to attract love. To make this refreshing tea, you're going to need:

* Mandarin oranges (one or two small ones)
* Sugar (two tablespoons)
* Cinnamon (two sticks)
* Hibiscus flowers (three tablespoons)

Boil five to six cups of water, turn off the heat, add the hibiscus and cinnamon, cover, and let it sit for 20 minutes. Add the sugar and oranges to a pitcher, strain the tea into it, and stir. Serve with ice.

Calming Cold Brew

A cold moon brew is very calming and relaxing, perfect for a summer night. To make it, you'll need one tea bag of each of the following:

* Lavender
* Lemon balm
* Chamomile

Fill a glass bottle with the above ingredients and four cups of hot water, tightly close, and leave it under the moonlight until it cools down. Then, strain and enjoy.

Floral Tea

Floral tea smells great on a summer night because of all the different flowers it has. It's perfect for a night in the garden. To make it, you'll need:

* A little honey
* Cornflower (a pinch)
* Passionflower (a pinch)
* Hibiscus (a pinch)
* Jasmine (a pinch)
* Lavender (a pinch)
* Rose petals (a pinch)
* Lady Gray or Earl Gray (two teaspoons)

Combine the tea and flowers and add two cups of boiling water. Let it steep for two to four minutes, strain, and serve either hot or cold.

Summer Tea

This blend can be enjoyed on a summer morning, as it'll give you lots of energy. The ingredients you're going to need are the following:

* Eucalyptus leaves
* Elderberry
* Hibiscus

Lightly mix all the ingredients and pour boiling water over them. Then, let it steep for five minutes, strain, add ice, and drink.

WHITE CLOVER BREW

A white clover iced tea has detoxifying properties and acts as a health tonic. For this brew, you'll need:

- Lemon wedge
- A little honey or maple syrup
- Fresh white clover blossoms (a cup)

Place the blossoms in a jar and pour four cups of boiling water over them. Let it steep for 30 minutes, strain, and serve over ice with honey/maple syrup and lemon wedge, if you wish.

FEMININE

This blend makes a mild-bodied and refreshing tea with a slightly sweet and spicy flavor that can help harmonize and bring balance to your body. Chaste Tree is not recommended for use with hormonal contraceptives. You'll need:

- Raspberry leaf
- Chaste tree berry
- Lemon verbena
- Linden flower and leaf
- Nettle leaf
- Cinnamon
- Lemon peel
- Stevia leaf

Simply mix equal parts of the ingredients and let the tea steep for about 10 minutes. Transfer it into a jug, add ice cubes and place it in the refrigerator to cool for 30 minutes.

Cozy Teas

Chocolate Tea

Hot chocolate is a very cozy drink for the fall, but pairing it with tea will take it to the next level. To make it, you're going to need half a cup of each:

* Cacao nibs
* Dried mint leaves
* Pu-erh tea

Lightly combine the ingredients and use a tablespoon for every cup of water. Store the rest in a jar and tightly close.

Cinnamon Blend

A cinnamon blend will warm you up and relax you at the same time on a cozy night. To make it, you'll need the following herbs:

* Oat straw leaves and stem (a tablespoon)
* Shredded licorice root (a pinch)

Bring a cup of water to a boil and place a teabag with the herbs in it. Leave it for ten minutes, strain, and drink.

Ginger Turmeric Comfort Blend

A ginger turmeric blend will keep you company when watching a movie on the couch, as it calms you down. To make it, you'll need the following:

* Turmeric root
* Fresh ginger
* Cinnamon stick
* Orange peel or a slice of apple

Simply boil water and pour it over the herbs. Let the tea steep for ten minutes, strain, and add the orange peel or apple slice if you wish.

Tulsi Herbal Blend

A tulsi herbal blend will relax you and help you adapt to stress in the beginning of the season. The ingredients you'll need are:

* A little honey
* Some lemon juice
* Dried orange peel (half a teaspoon)
* Dried ginger root (a pinch)
* Dried lemongrass (half a teaspoon)
* Turmeric (a pinch)
* Dried tulsi (a teaspoon)

Bring a cup of water to a boil and pour it over a tea bag that contains the orange peel, ginger, lemongrass, and turmeric. Leave it for ten minutes, strain, and add the lemon juice and honey.

Vanilla Blend

This blend is very sweet and slightly energizing and will instantly cozy you up. To make it, you'll need:

* Shredded toasted coconut (a teaspoon)
* Dried elderflower (a teaspoon)
* Vanilla extract or powder (half a teaspoon)
* Red rooibos leaves (a teaspoon)

Lightly mix the rooibos, coconut, and elderflower together and pour a cup of boiling water over it. Leave it for ten minutes, strain, and add the vanilla extract.

Winter Sun Lemon Tea

A sun tea will keep you warm in the winter days. To make it, you're going to need:

* Black pepper (a pinch)
* Cinnamon powder (half a teaspoon)
* Turmeric powder (half a teaspoon)
* Some lemon juice
* Ginger (an inch)

Start by finely grating the ginger and mixing it with the rest of the ingredients. Then, warm up (don't boil) a cup of water and pour over the ingredients. After that, let the tea steep for ten minutes under the sun.

Yin Tea

A Yin blend acts as a tonic for the female reproductive system and also has a relaxing effect. To make it, you'll need the following:

- A little honey
- Some coconut milk
- Dried rose buds (three to five)
- Dried shatavari root (a tablespoon)
- Dried white peony root (a tablespoon)

Heat two cups of water on high heat, along with the shatavari and peony, and when it boils, cover it. Simmer on low heat for 40 minutes. Then, remove from the heat, add the rose buds, and cover for five minutes. Finally, strain, add the coconut milk and the honey, and enjoy.

Morning Brews

Boost Blend

A boost tea will fill you with the energy and motivation you need to start the day. To make it, you'll need:

* Black tea (a tea bag)
* Sage leaves (about one or two)
* Fresh rosemary (two sprigs)
* Orange peel
* Cinnamon stick (about one or two)
* A little honey
* A little almond milk

Boil some water, pour it over the herbs, and leave it for four minutes. Then, add the tea and leave it for two to three minutes. After that, strain, add the honey and almond milk, and enjoy.

Soothing Tea

This blend will soothe and energize you, so that you can go about your day feeling calm and uplifted. To make it, you'll need:

* A little honey
* Lemon slices (about two)
* Dried lavender flowers

Heat some water, add the lavender flowers, and leave them for five minutes. Then, strain, squeeze the juice from the lemon slices, and leave them inside. After that, add the honey and enjoy.

Pure Morning Blend

A cup of this herbal blend in the morning will instantly boost you. To make it, you're going to need:

* Apple leaves
* Mint
* Moringa

Simply pour boiling water over the ingredients and let the tea steep for about ten minutes. Then, strain and enjoy.

Uplifting Tea

An uplifting tea will boost your mood so that you're ready to seize the day. The ingredients you'll need are the following:

- A little honey
- Dried lemon peels
- Earl Gray
- Sun water

Boil a cup of sun water, pour it over the Earl Gray and lemon peels, and let it steep for five minutes. After that, add honey and stir clockwise while chanting. Imagine you are being filled with sunbeams with each sip.

Energizing Potion

An energizing potion will make you feel refreshed, energized, and concentrated for the day ahead of you. To make this potion, you're going to need:

- A little honey
- A crushed cardamom pod
- A pinch of grated lemon zest
- A pinch of chopped ginger root
- A cinnamon stick
- A tea bag of green tea
- Sun water (a cup)

To make sun water simply fill a bottle with water, close tightly, and leave it outside during daytime to charge it. About four hours is enough. Start by lightly mixing the tea and herbs and add the boiling sun water. Let it steep for about five minutes. Then, strain, add honey while stirring clockwise with the cinnamon stick, and drink.

Tea with a Witch

Cottage Witch Rose Tea

This tea smells amazing and will instantly relax you. The ingredients are:

* Dried cranberries (a tablespoon)
* Rosebuds (four tablespoons)

Start by chopping the rosebuds and mixing them with the cranberries. Then, pour four cups of boiling water over the mixture, steep for five minutes, strain, and drink.

Forest Witch Tea

A forest tea will help you connect with the energies of the earth. To make it, you'll only need:

* Crushed honeysuckle flowers (two or three cups)
* A little honey

Boil two cups of water and simply pour it over the honeysuckle. Then, let it steep for ten minutes, strain, add honey, and enjoy.

Kitchen Witch Herbal Tea

A honey herbal tea can help you relax and unwind after a long day. To make it, you're going to need:

* Dried blueberries (a teaspoon)
* A cinnamon stick
* Honey (a teaspoon)
* Chamomile (two tablespoons)

Lightly mix your ingredients and pour four cups of boiling water. Afterwards, let the tea stand for five minutes, strain, add the honey, and enjoy.

Moon Witch Lavender Tea

A lavender tea will connect you with lunar energies and is especially good for spells involving the Moon. The ingredients include:

* Mint leaves (a cup)
* Dried lavender petals (four tablespoons)

Add your ingredients to four cups of boiling water, strain, and enjoy. Add a little honey if you wish.

Sea Witch Healing Tea

Drinking tea is directly associated with the energies of water. To make this healing tea, you'll need:

- A couple of lemon slices
- Dried nettles (two tablespoons)
- Chopped orange peel (two tablespoons)
- Hibiscus tea (two tablespoons)

Boil five cups of water and pour it over the ingredients. Leave the tea for five to six minutes, strain, add the lemon slices, and serve.

Hedge Witch Green Tea

A green tea with cinnamon will give you energy and help you connect with the spirits of the earth. The ingredients are:

- Lemon zest (half a teaspoon)
- Ginger (half a teaspoon)
- Two cinnamon sticks
- Green tea (four tablespoons)

Bring four cups of water to a boil and pour it over the mixture of the ingredients. Let it steep for three to five minutes, strain, and enjoy.

Witchy Brews

Faery Tea

If you're into Faery magic or working with the Fae, this brew can help you see them clearly, and its ingredients are associated with the Fae. You'll need the following:

* A little honey
* Lemon juice (half a teaspoon)
* Dried rosemary (a teaspoon)
* Lavender (a teaspoon)

Bring a cup of water to a boil, pour it over the herbs, and let it steep for at least five minutes. Strain, add the lemon juice and honey, and drink.

Altmer-style Tea

This ginger rose tea can be served either hot or cold. To make it, you'll need:

* Dried hibiscus tea (a teaspoon)
* Dried rose petals (five to eight)
* Sugar (a cup)
* Two large ginger roots

Start by peeling and slicing the ginger roots. Then, bring two and a half cups of water to a boil, add the ginger and sugar, and let them boil for five minutes. Then, remove the mixture from the heat, add the hibiscus and rose petals, and cover the pot until it cools down. After that, strain and serve.

Divination Tea

Most people in the witchcraft community practice divination and, mainly, tarot reading. This tea recipe is specifically designed to enhance psychic and prophetic abilities, as well as make a connection with spirit guides easier. To make this tea, you'll need the following:

* Rose hip (a tablespoon)
* Mugwort (a tablespoon)
* Eyebright (a teaspoon)
* Lemon balm (two tablespoons)
* Irish breakfast, English breakfast, or Chinese black tea (two tablespoons)

Lightly blend the herbs and use a teaspoon of the blend for every cup of water. Pour boiling water over the herbs and let the tea steep for about two or three minutes. Then, strain and drink.

Protection, Harmony & Prosperity

This was one of my first proper attempts at tea magic, and I felt really good about it. I remember it was a gloomy, grey, rainy day, but as soon as I'd drained the last drops of my tea, the sun shone straight through my windows. If you don't have a cup or mug in a color that matches your intentions, use a plain white one.

WHAT YOU NEED:

- White tea for cleansing, protection (also a good antioxidant)
- Rose petals for harmony, concentration, protection, and beauty
- Chamomile for peace, hope, happiness, prosperity, and harmony
- Mint for joy, protection, prosperity, success, joy, and purification
- Orange teacup for protection, success, confidence, strength, prosperity, happiness, and inspiration

WHAT'S NEXT:

1. Add the ingredients to the infuser and steep in hot water for 5 minutes

2. Pour out your first cup. Bring the cup to your face and close your eyes, breathing in the aromas and recite three times.

    "I feel protected, I live in harmony, I am prosperous"

3. Take your first sip and feel the tea travel through you with your intentions.

4. Now saying any other intentions/affirmations corresponding to the ingredients you may want to manifest out loud and take a sip in between each one (but be careful not to finish the cup yet!). For example: *I am harmonious* \sip\ *I am protected* \sip\ *I am cleansed* \sip\ *I am prosperous* \sip\ *I am hopeful* \sip\ *I am successful* \sip\ *I am beautiful* \sip\

5. Repeat the first another three times before finishing the tea. While focusing on the tea infusing you with your intentions as it moves through your body.

6. Enjoy the rest of the pot of tea!

First Aid Tea Spell

There is a big difference between drawing in spirits' help and understanding them. This tea spell will help you improve your psychic development and call forth on the spirits. It is important to note that calendula, for me, is very powerful. It is up to you how much you want to use, but I can't guarantee the taste while increasing the amount.

WHAT YOU NEED:

* Rosemary (a teaspoon) for healing, purification, love and protection
* Parsley (half a teaspoon) for protection, mental powers, purification and healing
* A very small pinch of calendula for divination, remembrance and honor
* One light squeeze of a lemon for love and purification
* Honey (a tablespoon)

WHAT'S NEXT:

1. Add the ingredients to the strainer and steep in hot water for 5 minutes
2. Squeeze the lemon and add the honey
3. Stir clockwise and, keeping your eyes closed and visualizing a glow around the cup, say the following chant:

    "My arms are open to the beyond,

    my eyes are open to my friends.

    I ask for the guidance of those who know

    the warmth of life and caress of death."

4. Drink and feel the energy moving through you until the glow begins to create a shape. It can be the sprinkle of light through the forest or a smoky haze as the sun shines through the fog; it depends on the element you connect to.
5. Take a couple of deep breaths, relax your body and open your eyes.

Flying Potion

Even though this potion won't make you fly literally, it can help you with lucid dreaming, hedge riding, and astral traveling. To make it, you'll need a pinch of each of the following dried herbs:

* Mint
* Mugwort
* Wormwood

Start by chopping the dried herbs first and then mix them lightly. Pour boiling water over them, let the tea steep for about five minutes, strain, and drink. You can add honey if you wish. Make sure you do your own research or consult a healthcare professional before consuming this tea, as mugwort and wormwood are known to have serious negative side-effects.

Herbal Clairvoyance Tea

An herbal clairvoyance blend is useful for enhancing your psychic abilities and, especially, clairvoyance. To make this tea, you'll need:

* Mugwort
* Bay
* Nutmeg
* Cinnamon
* Rose petals

Lightly mix one part of each of the first four herbs and three parts of the rose petals. Place them in a teapot with boiling water, cover, and let the tea steep for a few minutes. Then, strain and drink.

Herbal Psychic Tea

This psychic tea will enhance your psychic abilities and amplify divinatory practices. To make it, you'll need to mix a teaspoon of each of the following herbs:

* Orange peel
* Celery seeds
* Anise seeds
* Cinnamon powder
* Jasmine
* Peppermint
* Mugwort

Lightly mix all the herbs and pour boiling water over them. Then, let it steep for 10 to 15 minutes, strain, and drink.

Potion for Astral Projection

Astral traveling is a common practice among the witchcraft community, but it's often very hard to achieve. Although this potion won't make you astral travel instantly, it'll aid your practice and make it a bit easier for you to do that. To make it, you'll need:

* A little honey
* Cardamom
* Cloves
* Cinnamon
* Black tea

Mix the ingredients in equal parts and pour boiling water over the mixture. Let it steep for about five minutes, strain, add honey, and drink.

Protection Potion

This is a very good protection potion that will ward off evil and negative energy. The ingredients you'll need include:

* A little maple syrup
* Orange juice from one orange
* Pine needles
* Chai tea

Place the chai tea bag inside your cup and add the pine needle and orange juice. Then, pour some boiling water over the ingredients and let the tea steep for five minutes. After that, add the maple syrup and stir counterclockwise for banishing negativity or clockwise for attracting positivity and protection. If you wish, you can charge your tea by placing your cup next to smoky quartz and obsidian, while holding it in your hands and visualizing an energy shield forming around you, protecting you from negativity.

Enhancing Spiritual Awareness & Power

A spiritual awareness tea is best consumed before rituals related to spiritual awareness or divination. The ingredients you'll need are:

* Clove (two teaspoons)
* Cinnamon powder (two teaspoons)
* Yarrow root (a tablespoon)
* Thyme (a tablespoon)
* Rose petals (two tablespoons)

Start by lightly mixing the herbs together and boiling a cup of water. Then, pour the water over the mixture, let it steep for 20 minutes, strain, and drink.

Prophetic Dreams

If you're into dream work, this tea will enhance psychic dreams. To make it, you'll need the following ingredients:

* Cinnamon (half a teaspoon)
* Mugwort (a teaspoon)
* Peppermint (a teaspoon)
* Chamomile (a teaspoon)
* Rose petals (two teaspoons)

Lightly mix the ingredients and pour boiling water over a teaspoon of the mixture. Let it steep for about five minutes and chant. Then, strain and drink. It's best if you drink this tea 30 minutes before going to bed.

Psychic & Divination Work

A psychic and divination blend is designed to enhance your psychic powers and expand visions. To make it, you'll need:

* Mugwort (three teaspoons)
* Yarrow (a teaspoon)
* Rose petals (a teaspoon)
* Cinnamon (a teaspoon)

Start by lightly mixing all the ingredients and use a tablespoon of the blend for every cup of water. Then, boil some water, pour it over the ingredients, and let it steep for about five minutes. Don't drink this tea if you are pregnant.

Vivid Dreams

Vivid dreams happen during the stages of deep sleep (R.E.M.) that help us feel well-rested and refreshed when we wake up. This tea will induce deep sleep and help you go to bed easier. Don't drink this tea if you're pregnant. To make it, you'll need:

* Dehydrated blueberries (a cup)
* Dehydrated raspberries (half a cup)
* Rose hips (half a cup)
* Mugwort (four tablespoons)
* Peppermint (four tablespoons)
* Holy basil (four tablespoons)
* Chamomile (four tablespoons)

Crush the blueberries and raspberries and lightly mix them with the rest of the ingredients. Use about one or two teaspoons per cup of tea, steep for five minutes, and consume before going to bed.

Banishing

This tea can banish conflicts or unwanted energies and can be drunk before casting a spell. To make it, you're going to need the following ingredients:

* Honey (two teaspoons)
* Three black peppercorns
* Black tea (a teaspoon)
* Chili powder (a pinch)
* Ginger (half of the nub)
* Three blackberries
* Two cinnamon sticks

Boil two cups of water and add the cinnamon, blackberries, ginger, black tea, peppercorns, and honey. Then, dip your finger into the chili powder and add it to the tea by rubbing your index finger with your thumb. Leave the tea for about three to five minutes, strain, and drink. If you want to enhance the effects of the spell, you can charge the tea with tourmaline or a black candle, use moon water, and tie a red cord on the mug.

Tea Curse

This is a powerful tea curse that can't be reversed, so it's better if used with caution because the person drinking it will have a very hard time for about a month. To make this potion you're going to need:

* Mullein (two teaspoons)
* Cayenne pepper (a teaspoon)
* Black salt (a teaspoon)
* Black chalk (one thirtieth of a teaspoon or a very small pinch)
* Black tea (two tea bags)
* Sugar (a cup)
* Medium ripe peaches (two)
* Fresh strawberries (a cup)

Start by lighting a black candle and mixing together with a cup of water the black chalk, mullein, pepper, black salt, sugar, strawberries, and peaches. Then, boil on low heat until the ingredients are melted, remove from the heat, and let it cool. Afterwards, let the black tea steep in eight cups of boiling water for five minutes. Finally, combine the tea with the mixture, place it in a pitcher, refrigerate it, and give it to the person you wish to curse.

Gratitude Tea

There is an abundance of things to be grateful for, and those are the blessings we should count every day, even when afraid that the walls may come tumbling down. To make this tea, you'll need:

- Dried tulsi leaf (a teaspoon)
- Dried dandelion root (a teaspoon)
- Grated ginger (half a teaspoon)

Lightly mix your herbs and pour boiling water over them. Then, let the tea steep for five minutes, strain, sip, and feel the gratitude radiating from your heart. Maybe you will be able to skip ahead to the happy ending.

Ancestor Tea

This tea helps you connect with your witch allies and to give them a most welcome offering. You'll need:

- Mugwort (a teaspoon)
- Mint (half a teaspoon)
- Yarrow (a teaspoon)
- Juniper berries (13)

The specific amounts used will vary based on your unique constitution as with all botanical medicine. However, the above quantities steeped in two cups of boiled water are a good formulary for most of us.

Wheel of the Year

Wild Hunt Tea

A Wild Hunt tea is very warm and aromatic. In other words, perfect for snuggling during the winter solstice or Yule. To make it, you'll need:

* Elderflower (a teaspoon)
* Mint (a teaspoon)
* Ginger (two teaspoons)
* Two orange peels
* Cocoa (three teaspoons)
* Cinnamon (two teaspoons)
* Sage (two teaspoons)
* Black tea with toffee (two teaspoons)
* White tea (a tablespoon)

Lightly mix together the ingredients and use one or two teaspoons per cup of tea. Let it steep for about three to five minutes, strain, and enjoy.

Tea for the Awakening of Demeter

Demeter tea is best consumed on the transition between winter and spring (Imbolc), as it's refreshing and warm at the same time. The ingredients you'll need are:

* Fennel seeds (half a teaspoon)
* Citronella (a teaspoon)
* Jasmine flowers (two teaspoons)
* Orange blossom flowers (a teaspoon)
* Basil (a teaspoon)
* Lavender (two teaspoons)
* Sage (a teaspoon)
* Green tea (two teaspoons)
* White tea (three teaspoons)

Lightly mix all the ingredients and use one or two teaspoons of the blend per cup of tea. Let it steep for five minutes, strain, and drink.

Chasing the Hare Tea

Spring equinox or Ostara needs a blend that celebrates nature's blooming beauty of this season. To make it, you're going to need:

* Heather flowers (three teaspoons)
* Cinnamon (two teaspoons)
* Dehydrated apple (two slices)
* Orange blossom (a teaspoon)
* Jasmine flowers (one and a half teaspoons)
* Sage (a teaspoon)
* Green tea (three teaspoons)

Lightly mix all the ingredients together and use one or two teaspoons per cup of tea. Let it steep for about five minutes, strain, and drink.

Walpurgis Night Tea

This Walpurgis blend smells and looks like a field of flowers, which is the perfect place to drink it and celebrate the end of spring or Beltane. To make it, you'll need the following:

* Calendula (two teaspoons)
* Cinnamon powder (a teaspoon)
* Lavender (a teaspoon)
* Jasmine (two teaspoons)
* Rose petals (two teaspoons)

* Sage (half a teaspoon)
* Green tea (three teaspoons)
* Red tea (two teaspoons)

Lightly mix the above ingredients. To make the tea, use one or two teaspoons of the blend per cup of tea. Let it steep for about five minutes, strain, and enjoy.

The Greenman Tea

The Greenman blend is suitable for summer solstice or Litha, because it'll relax and refresh you at the same time. To make it, you're going to need the following:

* Calendula (a teaspoon)
* Two lemon peels
* Cinnamon powder (a teaspoon)
* Rosemary (half a teaspoon)
* Sage (a teaspoon)
* Lavender (two teaspoons)
* Black tea (a teaspoon)
* Red tea (three teaspoons)

Simply mix all the ingredients, pour hot water over them, and let the tea steep for five minutes. Then, strain, let it cool down, and enjoy over ice.

Dancing at Lughnasadh

A Lughnasadh blend is good for an end-of-summer celebration and for giving thanks to Nature, for all the goods she gave you. For this blend, you'll need the following ingredients:

* Dried apple (a slice)
* Heather (two teaspoons)
* Calendula (one and a half teaspoons)
* Lavender (two teaspoons)
* Lemon beebrush (two teaspoons)
* Cinnamon powder (a teaspoon)
* Sage (half a teaspoon)
* Black tea (a teaspoon)
* Green tea (two and a half teaspoons)

Lightly mix the herbs and use one or two teaspoons per cup of tea. Let it steep for five minutes, strain, and enjoy.

Dionysus Blend

A Dionysus blend will give you the vibes of fall equinox or Mabon, as it's both warm and solid, plus you can drink it either hot or cold. To make it, you'll need the following herbs:

Clove buds (half or one teaspoon)
* Rose petals (a teaspoon)
* Cinnamon pieces (two teaspoons)
* Rose hip (two teaspoons)
* Ceylon black tea (a tablespoon)

Lightly mix the herbs and use one to two teaspoons per cup of tea. Let it steep for about five minutes, strain, and enjoy. If you wish, you can add honey and/or any type of milk.

All Hallows' Eve Tea

The following blend combines fall and Samhain energies perfectly, as it's both aromatic and bold. To make it, you're going to need the following:

* Sugar (a tablespoon)
* Lavender (a tablespoon)
* Cinnamon powder (a teaspoon)
* Vanilla extract (a tablespoon)
* Three apples

Cut the apples into slices and remove the core. Put the slices in a blender, cover them with water, and blend them. Then, add the puree to a french press or cheese cloth and filter it out. Pour the cider, vanilla, cinnamon, and sugar into a saucepan and heat it. Once the mixture is heated, pour it into a cup and add the lavender. Leave it for three to five minutes and enjoy.

Elixiers

Anti-Anxiety Tea

An anti-anxiety tea will keep you company in your self-care moments and it'll relax you. The ingredients you'll need are:

* A little honey
* Dried lemon thyme (a tablespoon)
* Dried mint (a tablespoon)

Lightly mix the herbs and pour boiling water over them. Let it steep for five minutes, strain, and enjoy.

Antibacterial Tea

An antibacterial tea can help with mucus in the lungs and will boost your immune system. To make it, you'll need:

* Clove (a pinch)
* A cinnamon stick
* Fresh ginger (half an inch)

Place the ingredients in a pot and add three cups of water. Once the water boils, reduce to medium heat and leave it for five minutes. Then, strain and drink.

Bloating Tea Recipe

It's known that too much salt can cause water retention, which will make you feel bloated. This recipe contains herbs that will help your body get rid of extra salt and water, like:

* Hibiscus flower
* Nettle leaf
* Ginger root
* Elderflower
* Elderberry
* Black cumin
* Green tea

Simply mix equal parts of the ingredients and let the tea steep for about 10 minutes. However, don't drink this tea if you're pregnant, breastfeeding, have low blood pressure, diabetes, or kidney problems.

Calming Tea

This calming tea will relax you if you're going through a stressful period. To make it, you'll need:

* Monn water
* Dried lavender petals (a tablespoon)

To make it, start by boiling a cup of moon water and adding the lavender petals. Then, steep for five minutes, strain, and add some honey, while stirring clockwise.

Damp Cough Tea

A damp cough tea can effectively alleviate the symptoms of bronchitis. To make it, you'll need:

* Crystallized ginger root (three pieces)
* Marshmallow root (a tablespoon)
* Cinnamon sticks (three)
* Black peppercorns (30)
* Fennel seeds (a teaspoon)
* Anise stars (four)
* Cloves (20)
* Cardamom pods (30)
* Black tea (four teaspoons)

Fill a pan with four or five cups of water and add all the ingredients, simmering for five minutes. Then, turn off the heat and leave it for another ten minutes. Finally, strain and drink.

Digestive Help

A tea such as this one will enhance and soothe your digestive system. To make it, you'll need:

* Cumin seeds (a tablespoon)
* Dried ginger (a tablespoon)
* Fenugreek seeds (two tablespoons)
* Coriander seeds (two tablespoons)
* Fennel seeds (two tablespoons)

Lightly combine the herbs and use a teaspoon per cup of tea. Start by adding the herbs and a cup of water to a saucepan, and simmer it on low heat, covered, for 20 minutes. Then, simply strain and drink.

Elderflower Tea for a Fever

An elderflower tea can prevent a cold and help the body release toxins during a fever. To make it, you'll need the following:

* A little honey
* Raspberries (two or three)
* Some fresh mint
* Dried yarrow leaves (four tablespoons)
* Dried elderflowers (half a cup)

Boil three cups of water and steep the yarrow leaves and elderflowers for five to six minutes. Then, add the raspberries, honey, and mint for another two minutes, strain, and enjoy.

Fever Summer Tea

This summer tea will reduce a fever and relax you at the same time. To make it, you'll need:

* Any type of milk
* A little honey
* Some lemon juice
* Turmeric or ginger powder (a pinch)
* Herbal tea bag

Fill half of your mug with boiling water and brew your herbal tea for five minutes. Then, strain, add the rest of the ingredients, and enjoy.

Glowing Hair and Skin Herbal Tea

A blend for the hair and skin will make both healthier, due to all the vitamins and minerals it contains. The ingredients include:

* Cinnamon chips (a teaspoon)
* Oat straw (two teaspoons)
* Nettle leaves (two teaspoons)
* Rose petals (three teaspoons)
* Raspberry leaves (a tablespoon)
* Spearmint leaves (two tablespoons)
* Horsetail (two tablespoons)

Lightly mix all your herbs together and use two teaspoons per cup of boiling water. To make a tea from this blend, pour boiling water over the herbs and let it steep for 15 to 30 minutes. Then, simply strain and drink.

Headache Remedy

Honey green tea is known to relieve migraines and headaches. To make this tea remedy for a headache, you'll need:

* A little honey
* Green tea (a tea bag)
* Fresh turmeric (a teaspoon)
* Black pepper (a pinch)

Steep the green tea, turmeric, and pepper for three minutes in a cup of hot (not boiling) water. Then, strain, add the honey, and drink.

Immunity Blend

An immunity-boosting blend will help you get through the winter with a strong immune system. The ingredients for this blend include:

* Dried yarrow (half a teaspoon)
* Reishi powder (half a teaspoon)
* Dried ginger (a teaspoon)
* Dried rosehip (a teaspoon)
* Dried rose petals (two teaspoons)
* Dried elderberry (two teaspoons)

Lightly mix your ingredients and use three teaspoons per cup of tea. Pour boiling water over three teaspoons of the blend, cover, and let it steep for ten minutes. Then, strain and enjoy.

Mint Tonic Tea Recipe

A mint tea is known for boosting concentration and memory, both of which are especially needed before a study session. To make it, you'll need the following ingredients:

* Sage leaves (two teaspoons)
* Holy basil leaves (a tablespoon)
* Spearmint leaves (two tablespoons)

Boil two cups of water and pour it over a mixture of the herbs. Then, cover, steep for 15 minutes, strain, and drink.

Pain Relief Tea

Pain relief tea might take some time to have an effect, but it can effectively alleviate pain. To make it, you're going to need:

* A little honey
* Ginger
* Cinnamon
* Elderberry
* Thyme
* Bay leaf
* Lemon balm
* Peppermint
* Any tea as base

Simply brew the tea of your choice and add the rest of the herbs after you've mixed them. Then, strain, add some honey, and drink.

Period Cramps Tea

Tea is a great natural remedy for period cramps. To make it, you'll need:

* Honey (a teaspoon)
* Ginger (half a teaspoon)
* Chamomile (half a teaspoon)
* Lavender (half a teaspoon)

Boil a cup of water, add the ginger, and simmer it for two to five minutes. Then, remove from the heat, add the rest of the herbs and steep for one or two minutes. Afterwards, strain, add the honey, and enjoy.

Period Pain Moon Tea

Since the menstrual cycle is associated with the phases of the moon, a moon tea can also effectively alleviate period pain. To make this tea, you'll need a teaspoon of each of the following:

* Yarrow flowers or leaves
* Hibiscus
* Raspberry leaves
* Silverweed leaves
* Lady's mantle leaves

Lightly mix the herbs and add them to two cups of boiling moon water. Then, leave them for 10 minutes, strain, and drink during your period or five days before to prevent cramps.

Sickness-Healing Tea

Drinking this tea can help with symptoms of a cold or a flu. The ingredients include:

* Lemon juice (a tablespoon)
* Grated fresh ginger (one and a half teaspoons)
* Honey (a teaspoon)
* Cinnamon powder (a teaspoon)

Start by mixing together the honey and cinnamon until they form a paste and add the ginger and lemon juice. Then, warm up half a cup of water, pour it over the mixture, and let it sit under the sun for ten minutes.

Tea for a Cold

A tea for colds will immediately alleviate symptoms of a cold and will give you energy. The ingredients are:

* Yarrow (two teaspoons)
* Honey (two teaspoons)
* Lemon juice (from one lemon)
* Sage herbal tea (two or three teaspoons)
* Mint leaves (about five)
* A little chopped ginger

Lightly mix the ingredients and cover with boiling water. Then, let it steep for 15 minutes, remove the sage and yarrow, and leave it for five more minutes. After that, add the lemon juice and honey, and enjoy.

Better Metabolism & Glowing Skin

This tea will boost your metabolism and reduce acne because it has anti-inflammatory properties. To make it, you're going to need:

* A little honey
* Roasted barley
* Dried roses
* Dehydrated lemon slices
* Fresh ginger
* Green tea

Warm up a cup of water (don't boil it) and add the ingredients in equal parts. Then, steep for five minutes, strain, add the honey, and enjoy.

FERTILITEA

This tea will boost your fertility and you can drink it hot or cold. You're going to need:

* Green tea leaves (half a cup)
* Red clover (a cup)
* Dried peppermint (a cup)
* Dried stinging nettle leaf (a cup)
* Red raspberry leaf (two cups)

Lightly mix all the ingredients and store them in a glass jar. If you want to drink it as a tea, add one fourth cup of the mixture to a tea/coffee press, add boiling water, cover, and let it steep for 10 minutes. Then, strain, add honey and a lemon slice (if you wish), and enjoy. If you want to drink it as an infusion, place half a cup of herbs into a mason jar with four cups of water. Cover tightly and let it steep at room temperature overnight. Then, strain and consume.

WEIGHT LOSS TEA

Weight loss teas don't make you lose weight directly but help with cravings. Drink once a day. The ingredients you'll need are:

* Fenugreek
* Yerba mate
* Gymnema

Mix all the ingredients in boiling water and let it steep for about five minutes. Then, strain and enjoy.

Spiritual Baths

Spiritual baths are a great way to cleanse your energy and get rid of lower frequencies that cause stress, sadness, and emotional pain. Essentially, they're rituals for washing away negativity and detoxifying. Adding natural ingredients like herbs and bath salts increases the effectiveness of cleansing your aura. Before you take a spiritual bath, you need to clean the bathroom and tub, and add candles of your choice or those corresponding to your intention. With that said, we're now going to look at a few recipes for making your bath spiritual.

~

Abundance — This abundance bath tea will bring you prosperity and abundance. Start with cleansing your tub by burning white sage. Then, fill it with water and add bay leaves, Himalayan salt, and chamomile. You can also place some citrine near you and imagine the things you want to attract in your life.

New Moon — The new moon is the time to set new intentions. To make a bath for it, you'll need rose petals, maqui berry powder, lavender oil, and epsom salt. Add your ingredients to the water and surround yourself with amethyst, clear quartz, and candles.

Beauty Cleanse — This beauty spell will give you a radiant glow of beauty. You'll need to add to your bath ground oats that will unclog your pores and gently massage your skin with them. Place some aquamarine or jade around you for maximum results.

Full Moon — During this phase, the energies of the moon are the highest, and it's an ideal time for introspection and letting go. Start this ritual by writing down on a piece of paper the things you want to let go of and burn or rip apart the paper. Then, add your favorite bath salts to the water and surround yourself with candles and crystals of your choice. When you're done with your bath, drain the tub, and imagine all the things you wrote on your list leaving your body.

Spiritual — This lavender bath tea is designed to bring you self-love. You're going to need rose petals, lavender essential oil, and epsom sea salt. Simply fill your tub and add a few drops of the essential oil, along with the other ingredients.

Self-Love — A self-love bath spell will make you feel cleansed and better about yourself. You'll need lavender bath salts, black tea leaves, mint leaves, and a few slices of lemon. Simply fill the tub with water and add all the ingredients while visualizing a stream of light flowing over you. If you wish, you may say some affirmations. You can also add some rose quartz around the tub and say '*I unconditionally love myself*.'

Conclusion

To conclude, tea is a magical and medicinal tool that has been used since antiquity. I find that just the process of making a cup of tea is on its own a spiritual self-care. I often hold the mug in my hands to feel its warmth and smell the tea before I take a sip. I also find that being grounded or in a meditative state amplifies this experience and makes my teatime even more mindful. I like to hold the mug in my hands and walk outside while I drink my tea or sit on the ground, as this makes me feel even more connected to nature. Tea also makes me feel connected to the seasons when I'm enjoying a cold brew on a hot summer day under the sun, or a hot cup of tea wrapped in blankets during the winter time. I love to sit with my tea and just be there, forgetting about phones that are ringing, notifications, or any other form of mental stimulation. Making tea-drinking a practice is a great way to spice up your magical practice and remain grounded and centered.

In this book you've learned all about tea and how to use it in your own practice, but the journey doesn't end here. Now that you know the basics, it's time for you to venture off on your own. Experimenting with the recipes here and making up your own will help you find out which teas and blends are right for your body and your practice. The reason that I love magical tea is that I can modify the recipe/blend according to the ritual, ceremony, or spell I'm performing. Tea is perhaps the most easy-to-personalize magic tool, and it's widely available. The tea potions, brews, blends, and baths I shared with you in this book are just the beginning of a journey towards Great Wisdom or the Source. This book paves the way towards your journey and I would encourage you to also search for yourself which herbs and teas should and can be incorporated into your personal practice. And remember that the Great Wisdom will come from within. Blessed Be!

Tea Recipes & Spells Index

Abundance & Money, 62

Afternoon Energizing Blend, 58

All Hallows' Eve Tea, 90

Altmer-style Tea, 79

Ancestor Tea, 86

Anti-Anxiety Tea, 91

Antibacterial Tea, 91

Anxiety & Stressful Situations Tea Spell, 65

Aphrodisiac Herbal Tea, 66

Banishing, 85

Banishing Negativity & Gaining Courage, 53

Better Metabolism & Glowing Skin, 96

Bloating Tea Recipe, 91

Blockage Remover, 44

Blue Moon Tea, 41

Boost Blend, 75

Broken Heart Sun Tea, 44

Calendula Brew, 69

Calming Cold Brew, 70

Calming Tea, 92

Calming Tea Blend, 52

Centering, 54

Chasing the Hare Tea, 88

Chakra Healing, 34

Chocolate Tea, 72

Cinnamon Blend, 72

Cleansing, 54

Confidence Boost, 45

Cottage Witch Rose Tea, 77

Courage, 47

Creativitea, 58

Damp Cough Tea, 92

Dancing at Lughnasadh, 89

Digestive Help, 92

Dionysus Blend, 90

Divination Tea, 79

Dream Potion, 57

Easy Black Tea Prosperity Spells, 61

Elderflower Tea for a Fever, 93

Empowerment Tea, 58

Energizing Potion, 76

Enhancing Spiritual Awareness & Power, 83

Faery Tea, 79

Faithful Lust, 68

Feminine, 71

Fertilitea, 97

Fever Summer Tea, 93

First Aid Tea Spell, 81

Floral Tea, 70

Flying Potion, 82

For Change, 63

Forest Witch Tea, 77

Friendship Recipe, 67

Full Moon Tea for Intuition & Grounding, 42

Gender Dysphoria, 59

Ginger Turmeric Comfort Blend, 72

Glowing Hair and Skin Herbal Tea, 93

Good Fortune, 47

Gratitude Tea, 86

Grounding Citrus Tea, 52

Happiness Potion, 45

Hard Day Potion, 45

Headache Remedy, 94

Healing Matcha, 53

Hedge Witch Green Tea, 78

Herbal Clairvoyance Tea, 82

Herbal Psychic Tea, 82

Higher Self Tea Blend, 53

Honey Milk Tea, 46

Honoring the Divine Feminine, 41

Tea Recipes & Spells Index

Hope Brew, 46
Iced Love Potion, 69
Ignite Your Inner Flame, 64
Immunity Blend, 94
Inner Voice & Intuition, 50
Joy & Inner Peace, 48
Kitchen Witch Herbal Tea, 77
Lavender Moon Milk, 42
Libido Tea, 66
Love Is in the Air Potion, 67
Love Yourself Herbal Blend, 49
Maiden Tea, 56
Meditation Herbal Tea, 64
Mental Focus, 62
Milk Tea for Better Sleep, 57
Mint Tonic Tea Recipe, 94
Moon Witch Lavender Tea, 77
Motivation, 63
New Moon Tea, 42
Pain Relief Tea, 95
Peach Iced Tea, 69
Period Cramps Tea, 95
Period Pain Moon Tea, 95
Positive Thoughts, 46

Potion for Astral Projection, 83
Productivitea, 59
Prophetic Dreams, 84
Protection, Harmony & Prosperity, 80
Protection Potion, 83
Psychic & Divination Work, 84
Pure Morning Blend, 75
Reflective Vibe, 62
Relationship Tea, 67
Relaxation, 63
Releasing Negativity Tea Spell, 55
Romance & Passion Tea, 68
Sea Witch Healing Tea, 78
Self-Love Booster, 50
Self-Love & Empowerment Tea Spell, 51
Self-Love Iced Tea, 50
Sexual Arousal, 66
Sickness-healing Tea, 96
Sleep Potion, 56
Soothe Agitation, 64
Soothing Tea, 75
Summer Joy Tea, 47

Summer Tea, 70
Sweet Dreams, 57
Tea Curse, 85
Tea for a Cold, 96
Tea for Emotional Exhaustion, 44
Tea for the Awakening of Demeter, 88
The Greenman Tea, 89
The Power to Succeed Tea Spell, 60
Truth Tea, 48
Tulsi Herbal Blend, 73
Uplifting Tea, 48
Uplifting Tea, 76
Vanilla Blend, 73
Vivid Dreams, 84
Walpurgis Night Tea, 88
Warm Your Spirit, 49
Waxing Moon Tea, 43
Weight Loss Tea, 97
White Clover Brew, 71
Wild Hunt Tea, 87
Winter Sun Lemon Tea, 73
Yin Tea, 74
Yogi Tea, 54
Zodiac Blends, 36

Thank you very much for taking the time to read this book. I hope it positively impacts your life in ways you can't even imagine.

If you have a minute to spare, I would really appreciate a few words on the site where you bought it.

Honest feedbacks help readers find the right book for their needs!

Phoebe Anderson

www.ingramcontent.com/pod-product-compliance
Lightning Source LLC
Chambersburg PA
CBHW081120080526
44587CB00021B/3684